UNSTOPPABLE

Being Fierce, Fearless, and Unf*ckwithable in Life and Business

ROCHEL MARIE LAWSON

FEATURING: NICOLE BATISTE, DR. NAILAH G. BERAKI, ROSALIND BERESFORD,
KEARN CROCKETT CHERRY, MEILIN EHLKE, JC GARDNER, TRINA HAMMACK, DOREEN HILLIER,
MELINDA HOLMES, HEATHER JONES, GURUTEJ KHALSA, BESSIE LEE-CAPPELL,
AURA E. MARTINEZ, KIMLE NAILER, VICKI NOETHLING, ANNA PEREIRA, DR. PAM PERRY,
DR. PAMELA J. PINE, LJ RASPLER, IRENE VAKSBERG, MELISSA A. WASHINGTON

UNSTOPPABLE

BEING FIERCE, FEARLESS, AND UNF*CKWITHABLE IN LIFE AND BUSINESS

ROCHEL MARIE LAWSON

FEATURING: NICOLE BATISTE, DR. NAILAH G. BERAKI, ROSALIND BERESFORD, KEARN CROCKETT CHERRY, MEILIN EHLKE, JC GARDNER, TRINA HAMMACK, DOREEN HILLIER, MELINDA HOLMES, HEATHER JONES, GURUTEJ KHALSA, BESSIE LEE-CAPPELL, AURA E. MARTINEZ, KIMLE NAILER, VICKI NOETHLING, ANNA PEREIRA, DR. PAM PERRY, DR. PAMELA J. PINE, LJ RASPLER, IRENE VAKSBERG, MELISSA A. WASHINGTON

Unstoppable

Being Fierce, Fearless, and Unf*ckwithable in Life and Business

Rochel Marie Lawson

©Copyright 2022 Rochel Marie Lawson

Published by Brave Healer Productions

Paperback ISBN: 978-1-954047-52-5

eBook ISBN: 978-1-954047-51-8

DEDICATION

I dedicate this book to my beautiful daughter Lauryn Alexis Marie Lawson. Without your words of wisdom, guidance, love, and grace, I would not have had the vision to create this project. Mommy loves you with all her heart.

DISCLAIMER

This book offers words of wisdom regarding physical, mental, emotional, and spiritual wellbeing and is designed for educational purposes only. You should not rely on this information as a substitute for, nor does it replace professional medical or business advice, diagnosis, or treatment. If you have concerns or questions about your health, business, or mental wellbeing, you should always consult with a physician, other healthcare professional, or business professional. Do not disregard, avoid or delay obtaining medical or business-related advice from your healthcare or business professional because of something you may have read here. The use of any information provided in this book is solely at your own risk.

Developments in research may impact the health, business, and life advice that appears here. No assurances can be given that the information contained in this book will always include the most relevant findings or developments with respect to the particular material.

Having said all that, know that the women here have shared their tools, practices, and knowledge with you with a sincere and generous intent to assist you on your journey to being fierce, fearless, and unstoppable in business and life. Please contact them with any questions you may have about the techniques or information they have provided. They will be happy to assist you further!

TABLE OF CONTENTS

INTRODUCTION

We usually think of being a fierce, fearless, and unstoppable woman as someone who has suffered many trials and tribulations in life and has succeeded despite all odds being against her. When you throw in being unf*ckwithable in business and life, that connotes the meaning that this woman is a badass. Although this may be true, when you dig deeper into the essence, it means a woman who has decided that no matter what, she's going to do what she wants to do, how she wants to do it, and with whom she wants to do it, despite the trials, challenges, and difficulties she may face.

We have all experienced challenges. The women who move forward despite the struggles on their path obtain priceless wisdom that would have never been possible had they decided not to move forward. In this day and age, many women and men understand that through struggle, the muscle of courage is exercised, and it's through this, we can gain resilience, strength, and tenacity. There is no growth or opportunity to realize our true potential without putting in the work. Every human on the planet has experienced struggle. The process of being born is a struggle. It's our first experience breaking through to get to something better to create the world we're meant to live in.

Imagine the unlimited possibilities that become available to you when you tap into the wisdom of women who've faced the challenges in life and succeeded in standing in their greatness. Imagine being able to tap into the knowledge of women who've climbed some of the highest mountains in life, survived painful experiences, and overcome their fears to step into their greatness on their path to bliss. Wouldn't it be nice to have a roadmap filled with wisdom and guidance on how to be that unstoppable and unf*ckwithable woman no matter what shows up in your life?

This book is intended to be the go-to book for women of all ages, no matter where they may be on their path. Whether it's guidance, inspiration, or being uplifted—whether it's the fire you need to push you forward to do what you are on this earth to do, I want this book to inspire, empower, guide, motivate and strengthen you to be that fierce, fearless, and unstoppable woman that the Divine created you to be.

Most importantly, I want this book to be about passing down a legacy of wisdom for the future generations of females in our lineage. I desire that these words of wisdom we may never be able to share with our daughters, granddaughters, and great-granddaughters guide them on their journey in life and keep them forever connected to us. The wisdom in this book will enable them to experience the challenges in life a bit more easily.

Women are the most powerful species on the planet. Without women, human life is impossible. I want us to begin to recognize and own this power and to understand that we genuinely are fierce, fearless, unstoppable, and unf*ckwithable, and what we need to do is allow the wisdom of the trailblazers before us to be utilized in our life.

When I think about women who are examples of what I want, I think about women like Harriet Tubman, Michelle Obama, Oprah Winfrey, Rosa Parks, Susan B. Anthony, Amelia Earhart, Malala Yousafzai, Marie Curie, Junko Tabei, Frida Kahlo, Katherine Johnson, Madam C.J. Walker, Katharine Graham, Bessie Coleman, Wilma Rudolph, Mary McLeod Bethune, Mamie Johnson, and Angela Davis to name a few.

These women had to go through some things to achieve their greatness. These women had to be fierce, fearless, unf*ckwithable, and unstoppable in life. This is what I desire for all women around the world.

We are not in this alone, women. We have each other. We have to recognize this factor and know that no matter what curve balls life throws at us, we have the wisdom and power to achieve great things. We can be fierce, fearless, unstoppable, and unf*ckwithable in life.

CHAPTER 1

UNLOCKING BLISS

BREAKING THROUGH FEAR TO LIVE YOUR DREAM LIFE

Rochel Marie Lawson, RN, AHP, CMS

*"Fear is a far more dominant force
in human behavior than euphoria."*

~Alan Greenspan, 2013

There is nothing more difficult in life than conquering fear. Fear is the one emotion that can create havoc and cause damage in all areas of life. Fear activates anxiety and worry that unleashes unnecessary pain, torture, and suffering on the mind, body, and spirit. These lethal combinations of emotions destroy health, wealth, wisdom, and happiness. They prevent us from living the life of our dreams.

The seductiveness about fear will lead you to believe it's not the cause of your turmoil when confronted. This emotion will have you acknowledge that you caused this imbalanced state manifested in your mind and body. The result is the chaos you're experiencing in your life. Fear is our only adversary. The ghost and destruction of this emotion reside in criticism, death, ill health, loss of love, poverty, and old age.

When we begin to understand that fear is just an illusion within our ego set up to protect us, we can eliminate the doubts, negative thoughts, and self-criticism that kill us from the inside out. It requires us to have faith, belief, and confidence, which vanquish, dissolve and dissipate all adverse results of fear. At this point, unlocking bliss goes from a possibility to a reality.

MY STORY

The eighth year of my life was pivotal for me, as I learned the devastating effects fear has on the mind and the body. This fear eventually led to me having a 17-year journey of getting my health, wellbeing, and bliss back to a state of equilibrium—free of pain, torment, and torture after suffering from a medically undiagnosed stress-induced ulcer.

When I was eight years old, I had my first encounter with real fear outside of my parents' discipline for misbehaving during this year. I did not share this story with anyone for many years because it was so personal and traumatizing. From this experience, I developed the strength to conquer all fear that showed up in my life.

Like any eight-year-old child headed back to school in the fall, I anticipated seeing all my friends and meeting my teacher. I loved going to school, and I loved learning new things. However, this year would be different. One day at the dinner table, two days before school was supposed to start, my mom looked at me and said, " Rochel Marie, you will be going to a different school this year."

Initially, I was confused and asked my mom, "Why?" However, questioning the adults in my life was not an option when I was growing up. She looked at me and said, "Because I said so." The day before school started, I was excited because I realized I would see my cousins at recess. They were like brothers to me, and I loved being with them.

The first day of school is when the torture began. A girl in my class decided to select me as the student she would intimidate, bully, push around, harass and scare. This girl was nine getting ready to turn ten, and I just turned eight. I was an average height for an eight-year-old girl, but I was skinny. The bully was much taller than me and outweighed me by at least 15 pounds.

The first week of school was tough. The bully began her initial assault. She would make a fist and point to me when the teacher had her back turned while writing on the chalkboard. She would stick her foot out and trip me as I walked to the water fountain at the back of the classroom. She would push me around at recess, pull my hair, and say, "If you tell anyone, the yard duties or the teachers, I'm going to punch you in the nose and give you a bloody nose, I'm going to scratch your eyes out, and I'm going to flush your head in the toilet. I'm going to beat you up till you bleed and cry."

I don't know why I was so afraid of this girl. I was growing up around boys, playing with them and fighting them. However, this girl frightened me to the core. By the second week of school, the real terrifying torture began. She started pushing me down at recess; she began to walk up to me and punch me in the stomach; and she spit on me in class, all with the threats of, "If you tell anyone, I will beat you up, and I will have my sisters and brothers beat you up as well. If you tell your cousins, I will have my brothers beat them up too." I still remember those words as if I'd heard them yesterday. However, they no longer cause fear and terror to run down my spine or cause pain in my gut.

Because I loved my cousins, I did not want to cause them any harm, so I stayed silent. I didn't fight back. Back in those days, if children exhibited terrible behavior such as fighting, talking back to a teacher, or being disruptive in class, they would be sent to the principal's office. They would get paddled, made to call their parents, and get suspended from school.

The wrath of my parents for misbehaving at school was far more traumatizing than dealing with the bully.

As the school year progressed, the torture got worse. I began to develop stomach aches and started complaining I didn't feel well and was too sick to go to school. My tummy aches became my go-to for being able to avoid the bully. And because I was an outstanding student, my grades didn't suffer, and no one paid attention at first. My grandmother mentioned that I was beginning to miss school due to my stomach aches and suggested a doctor examine me.

I embarked on an entirely new journey with my health and wellbeing. But that's another story.

As the school year progressed, the torture intensified, and the suffering became worse. The happiest times of that year in school were the weekends because I would be free from the fear of the bully's pain.

A conversation I had with my grandmother was the beginning to the end of my torture, pain, and suffering. I did not share anything happening to me at school with the bully. However, I asked her, "What do you do when you're afraid?" She looked at me and said, "When I'm scared, I telephone the Divine through prayer and ask for guidance, and I wait for the Divine to telephone me back through my intuition with the advice I need to move forward to conquer my fear. "

When I asked my grandmother what she meant by intuition, she told me, "It's the stuff you share with me that you know about people. You know their circumstances without knowing why you know it." She said, "It's when the Divine gives you information that comes from within you, and you just know by the feeling of the message that it is from the Divine." Then she smiled at me and said, "You share stuff like this with me all the time."

That response was a game-changer for me.

That night I began to telephone the Divine through prayer, asking for guidance on how I could conquer my fear.

It didn't take long for the Divine to respond to my prayers; however, the response was not occurring through my intuition. It was happening in the events occurring in my life.

The first time was when the teacher saw the bully try to trip me and called her out. Next, another student told the teacher what they witnessed the bully doing to me, and the teacher began paying more attention to the interaction between the bully and me. She made sure to keep her away from me while we were in class. Then I found out while eavesdropping on a conversation between my mom and my aunt that we would be moving to a new city and I would be going to a new school next year.

I was like, "YES! Thank you, Divine!"

Then it finally happened. One morning when I was telephoning the Divine with my prayer, I received a direct response through my intuition.

The message was, *face the bully fearlessly, and there will be no bully to face. She will go away on her own.*

I will never forget that day or that message because first, I wrote the date and the wisdom down in my diary, and second, when I went to school that morning, I was ready to face my fear of the bully. She approached me as soon as I arrived on the playground. She started her usual morning manner of pushing, teasing, calling me names, and laughing about it in front of the kids on the playground.

Instead of walking away in fear, angry that I didn't do anything, I stood there without moving. I walked closer to the bully and looked her in the face, and said to her, "If you touch me one more time, I'm going to punch you in your face." Then I balled up my fists.

It seemed like time had stopped and that it was just she and I on the playground. She looked at me and said, "I'm going to beat you up after school," and I said, "I don't think so." I never had a problem with the bully from that day forward.

The school year ended, we moved to a new city, and I started a new school in the fall. That was my first lesson on learning how to break through fear.

The Divine taught me how to break through fear and become the brave, bold, fierce, fearless, and unstoppable woman I am today.

My next lesson came many years after that eighth year of my life, but it's a lesson that challenged me in many areas.

"Face fear, greet it, and go with it until it matures into fearlessness, accomplishment, and satisfaction."

~Rochel Marie Lawson

At the age of 22, I started a business with my husband. We were both young and envisioned being successful. I pushed him, and he pulled me along in the spirit of harmony as we embarked on being entrepreneurs. We were the first people in our family to start a legal business.

We didn't have seed money to start the business, but we had determination, grit, and energy.

We started the business the same time I finished nursing school. I decided I would work as a registered nurse at night in the emergency department and help him run the business during the day.

The incredible beauty of it all was that the business obtained huge customers right away. We hired our first employee, and we were off and running being the entrepreneurs we desired to be.

Life was challenging, but somehow we made things work out. We made payroll, finished projects ahead of schedule, providing quality work, and made a name for ourselves in the telecommunications installation industry. Even though I was burning the candle at both ends, everything was going very well. It's amazing what you can do when you're young, energized with drive and ambition.

I loved working as an emergency registered/trauma nurse, and then I was confronted with a big decision. I could no longer burn the candle at both ends. By this time, we had two children, the complexity of running a business, working in a profession I loved, and raising two children. It took a toll on me.

I was getting very little sleep, and the hubby and I began to bicker over the littlest things.

Finally, it happened. An opportunity to take the business to a seven-figure status became a reality. It would require a lot more time from me than I had in my current state of living.

And then that dreaded fear set in. All I had been working so hard to achieve was here, but I was scared. I was scared we wouldn't have enough money, that we'd lose our clients, and appear as failures. I had to choose: give up nursing or give up my role in the business.

Once again, I telephoned the Divine and waited for the Divine to telephone me back.

The message was: *step into the greatness I have blessed you with;* you *must let go of one trapeze rope so that you can* grab *the other, for this is your next step on your path to unlocking bliss.*

At this moment, I realized: *to do the work I'm here to do, to serve those that need my help, I have to let go of nursing and step into fully being the fabulous business owner I am.*

But here is the beautiful part of breaking through that fear. I did not have to let go of nursing completely. I just had to let go of it in the capacity that I was working. The beauty in recognizing this freed my mind, body, and spirit tremendously. Many beautiful doors of opportunity opened up for me that would have never been made available to me had I not let go of fear to unlock my bliss.

The Divine had more lessons for me to learn about breaking through fear. These lessons included fear of criticism, death, ill health, loss of love, poverty, and old age.

The beautiful thing about the lessons I've learned regarding conquering fear is that I get to share them with you. I get to give you a gift of smashing through fear that was divinely given to me so you can begin unlocking your bliss from this moment forward. I get to share with you the gift bestowed upon me that has the power to end the destruction, pain, suffering, and torture that fear creates in your mind, body, and spirit.

"Sometimes, the only difference between a woman who has created a life of bliss for herself and the one who hasn't is that the first was brave enough to trust her intuition."

~Rochel Marie Lawson

THE TOOL

Fear robs you of all power, and you lose contact with the universal power supply. When this happens, you begin to attract more of what you fear into your life.

Your attention creates your reality, and whatever you put your attention on will manifest in your reality. As long as you keep giving your awareness to what you don't want, what you don't want will keep appearing.

The lesson related to your fears will appear in your life in more significant and more complex ways until you can confront and shatter all that frightens you.

To break through fear and unlock your bliss, the first thing you have to do is connect with your inner being, your true self, and your eternal identity. When you awake to the good that resides within you, the realization that fear is not an enemy and the Divine utilizes every situation in our life for our highest good will become evident.

1. Telephone The Divine

Unlock the connection to the Divine by prayer. This is a crucial step because you cannot receive divine guidance without asking for divine guidance. If you never make the telephone call, you will never be able to make that connection. Even though the Divine knows what you require, it can't be granted if you don't communicate what you desire. The gift of free will is ask, and you shall receive. Stay silent, and the Divine won't hear you; there is no opportunity for you to experience divine guidance with silence.

2. Transmute Fear Into Faith

You cannot accomplish anything you cannot see yourself accomplishing. Fear is inverted faith that occupies precious space in your mind through a distorted mental picture, which brings to pass more of what you fear. When you let go of the burden of fear, the fire within you will burn through all of it and convert it into faith.

3. Master the Art of Thinking

When thinking about your fear, become a master thinker. The master thinker is an artist and is careful to paint only the divine designs of fierce, fearless, and unstoppable on the mind's canvas. The master thinker paints these pictures with masterly strokes of power and decision, having perfect faith that there is no power to distort their fearless perfection.

These three steps are the powerful beginning of how you can unlock your bliss and break through fear. To obtain a beautiful copy of the complete PDF and audio on how to unlock your bliss and break through fear, go to: www.blissfulliving4u.com/breakthroughfear

To become fearless, you must step out of your comfort zone. The truth is you must give up playing safe to increase your chances of living your dream life. Although this may sound frightening, sacrificing comfort is inevitable if you want to experience a life of bliss.

Wishing you a life filled with bliss.

Namaste,

Rochel Marie Lawson, RN, AHP, CMS

The Queen of Feeling Fabulous

Known as the Queen of Feeling Fabulous, **Rochel Marie Lawson** is a successful business owner, Registered Nurse, Ayurvedic Health Practitioner, Dream Lifestyle Transformation Facilitator, a multiple #1 Best Selling Author on Amazon, a 2-time International Best Selling Author and author of 4 other best selling books including "Intro To Holistic Health Ayurveda Style. She is a speaker, radio show hostess, and the president of Blissful Living 4 U, which was founded to bring wellness, wisdom, and wealth into the lives of individuals seeking a holistic path to living the life of their dreams.

Rochel Marie's energy, guidance, and enthusiasm have helped thousands of people improve their wellness, wisdom (aka mindset), and wealth by utilizing ancient, holistic principles that unlock the access for transformation to occur. She has been named one of the Top 50 Women-Owned Businesses in Silicon Valley and the creator of The Brave, Bold & Unstoppable Women's Summit.

Her weekly podcast, The Blissful Living Show, has been going strong for over ten years. She's been a guest writer for several blog publications and a featured core blogger for The Wellness Universe. She has been quoted in the Huffington Post and featured on Fox, CBS, NBC, and several other prominent media publication outlets.

Rochel Marie has spent over 25 years assisting people to achieve, elevate and sustain wellness and wealth through wisdom, to enhance the power of their minds, and to transform their lives with more abundance, clarity, energy, happiness, joy, peace, vitality, creativity, wisdom, prosperity, success and wealth. For more information, check out: www.blissfulliving4u.com

CHAPTER 2

RELATIONSHIP SUCCESS

A PATH TO TRUE SUCCESS AND FULFILLED LEGACY

Gurutej Khalsa, CEO

MY STORY

The two main ingredients of your life are energy and relationships. Without good energy, everything is hard. Relationships pervade every aspect of your life. Intimate ones, work ones, easy ones, challenging ones, children, neighbors, our homes which hold us—all of the things that we love or don't—are part of our relationship landscape.

Relationships are a vast and intricate subject. You're so intertwined in the relationships you know about and the relationships you take for granted—like your body parts and the floors and earth you walk on. Everything in your life is about whom or what you're in a relationship with: your finances, health, loves, regrets, successes, failures, and all human relationships. You're in a relationship with so much in your life, yet your most powerful relationship is you with you.

One of my most impactful and pervasive relationships started out quite strikingly. It was such an intricate and awe-inspiring teaching about the power of being connected deeply with yourself.

I started doing yoga in 1970 in a sweet, oleander encircled park in Tucson, Arizona. The yoga was so powerful it knocked me off my feet; with breathing that got me so high, I thought, *who needs drugs*. At that time, we all seemed to need drugs in our quest to "find God." The teacher played his guitar and chanted in a truly angelic, captivating voice at the end of class. I was hooked. I went every day, sometimes twice times a day.

So when our yoga teacher announced after class that there was a summer solstices celebration in Santa Fe, New Mexico, my sister and I looked at each other and said, "Lets go!" We figured we could drive out for the weekend. So we did in hopes of meeting "the yogi" whom we had heard so much about, including that he was the one who brought this yoga that we loved over from India.

After driving all Thursday night, we arrived tired and a little dazed. We were just in time to hear that the group was booted from the cool, pine ladened mountains above Santa Fe for not having a permit—hippies knew nothing of permits, nor did they care. The group relocated to a dry river gorge in the scorching sun. We questioned ourselves; *why had we driven all the way from Tucson for this?* However, we decided we were here, so let's just meet 'the yogi' we had heard so much about.

We did. There were only about 75 of us sitting out exposed to the harsh summer sun in our barely dressed hippie clothes when 'the yogi' came in regally, sat down on a rickety slapped-together wooden platform with black garbage bags suspended above him for shade.

Then the show began. He was amazingly charismatic, funny, and took us through a killer yoga set as he kept encouraging us at the top of his bellowing voice to, "Keep up and be kept up," meaning, hold the position and breakthrough instead of break down. He pushed us to do the thing we had come for—to be connected to the vastness of the all and the everything. We wanted that God connection, and he, in so many ways, told us he could and would deliver that.

We were sustained by the kindness of someone who brought us a truckload of watermelons; trust me, that is the perfect food in the desert and the scorching sun.

I loved the yoga because I got to bring my beautiful body into this Divine connection. I fell in love with this beautiful, graceful, powerful man of God.

Who would imagine that I would again attend a summer solstices celebration with "the yogi" one year later and never return to my home in Tucson? Instead, I would travel cross country, move into an ashram in a brownstone on Q street in Washington DC, far away from the vast skies and wildness of Tucson.

The yogi came to the DC ashram called Ahimsa, meaning peace. After the solstices week of celebration, where we did about 10-12 hours a day of yoga and meditation for ten days. We all got to spend time with him since there were only 100 of us sprinkled across America in those early days. Little did I realize what surrender meant at that time.

We dove into this lifestyle full force, no bungee cords, no catch nets. We brought our tattered longing with us. We got up at three am, did ancient yogic cleansing rituals, then yoga and chanting before a seven am breakfast, then scattered into the world to our callings or at least some job that brought in our rent money. My college training was put to use babysitting two young boys, then helping open the first vegetarian restaurant in DC called YES, where we often worked fasting on juices or water and cooking and serving those who weren't. It was fun being part of this shift at its roots.

The yogi gave us a life plan, and part of that was trust that he would match us up with the correct partner. There was no dialogue nor debate. You were either on for the total ride or you were off the train. This "match up" was not for tea or a date, but to marry from this day forward; a life partner. We figured we hadn't done such a good job picking our partners ourselves, so why not let someone who was older and wiser pick someone who would elevate us in our conscious search?

I bowed and said yes to his choice for me even though I had met the man and didn't even like him, much less feel any attraction towards him. Oh, and I had to move to Toronto. I had previously moved to Tucson because I hated cold. So this was a huge leap of faith for me on so many, many levels. Trust and surrender were the gifts that allowed this leap of faith.

But did trust and surrender all work out in the fairy tale style? Indeed not. It turns out that he, my husband, was a violent narcissist, which I should have recognized from my psychology training in college. But this was a different beast up close and personal. There we were in this cold and yes, foreign, country, two liberal arts majors running a spiritual community together without a handbook, without an effective communication strategy.

To say it was brutally challenging is an understatement. Yet, I held fast to the belief I could make it work because I gave my teacher, the yogi, my word that I would build a spiritual community here. We were the heads of this spiritual community and needed to "look good." The "look good" was more important than actually being good.

My most lasting memory of our relationship is where one of us was in the bathtub, and the other was sitting on the toilet; as we were trying to connect until the wee hours of the morning. We got up at three am, so 11-12 pm were the wee hours. I couldn't even tell you what we were talking about but I can tell you the feeling was spiraling into nowhere. Connection with him was like swirling spiraling energy pulling you into a swamp. It was a never-ending process with no resolution ever. Like bad sex, there was no ahh, ever.

Once, our yogi teacher described our communication as one talking high and one talking low. There is a crisscross but never a connection. This craziness got me to be a lifelong student of communication.

We long for a common union, and knowing how to achieve that connected state is one of the most important aspects of a successful relationship.

I will share how the yoga and morning meditations saved me; and it saved me from truly breaking down and going crazy. It put me in connection with my essence and fed my deepest self.

Was this a complete disaster? No, we had two gorgeous children, and I learned so many powerful lessons of both what to do and what not to do. My husband was what I now call a back door teacher. Ever had one of those? I learned what to pay attention to and, most of all, to never give up my intuition. Please pay attention when you lose your sense of humor and drown out or continuously second guess your intuition. This isn't going to end well. I remember when my then-husband called me to apologize for "the time he hit me." When I asked, "Which time?" He was floored, for he only remembered one of the many times. Amazing what we store in our memory banks and what we delete.

This gauntlet that I rode during the 15 years of this arranged marriage allowed me to help so many others see the unseen in their lives. Often, we are blind to so many aspects of ourselves. Truly, I remember going through crazy times thinking, remember this because this lesson, this pain, and this communication; you can use to help others through their challenges.

After 15 years in this vice grip of craziness, I got a direct download that I was complete. As I was walking behind my teacher's house in New Mexico, I literally saw this steel door descending, closing, and heard, *You are finished with this karma.* I knew what it meant. I should have felt this immense relief, but my first reaction was being stunned; that one vision and a couple of words broke the chains of so much pain on so many levels.

Did I blame my teacher for putting me through this? Yes, I did, and once I forgave him and myself, he called me and did something he rarely did, he apologized: "I am so sorry I married you to that man. He didn't deserve you."

"I already forgave you," I replied. "I learned so many things." By then, I had already unearthed many of the gifts I received from this relationship and didn't need his apology.

I remarried many years later to a wonderful soul who sees me and who honors me. Yes, we are two alphas in a bottle, so it's not always easy, but it's joyous and elevating, and we have a great sense of humor about things and occasionally ourselves too. We are consciously together to elevate each other.

With all this, I want to say it is my deep knowing that all relationships are set up and are arranged. They are arranged to unveil you. Sometimes with gentle, comforting love, and other times it feels as if you will never survive. I'm not advocating that staying to the bitter end or divorce; each relationship is different. Each relationship deserves a guide to help us unveil ourselves and our gifts.

Relationship is such a beautiful word; It's about learning to relate to each other. It's the ship that carries us through the rough and calm waters. That, plus understanding which means to stand under. We have the underpinnings of relationships. "Get real" is what they are calling us to do.

If you can remember to discern and not judge, it will serve and save you. What do I mean by that?

We see so much judgment these days. Judgment is you seeing something and analyzing it at the moment, putting it/them in a box, and never letting it out. It's both limited and static.

Someone hears or sees something and, without looking more deeply, reacts. We see part of the video clip that a specific TV station wants us to see in a particular light to keep us coming back for more crack. We often have the court of the internet and judge and sentence someone in the court of public opinion. Have you ever been part of the mob mentality?

Discernment means you pay attention to looking into a person, place, or thing with a neutral mind and seeing beneath the surface. You are willing to research, see into and keep your master view evolving. Give them the benefit of not the doubt but the benefit of the there may be more to this. This is priceless in all your relationships.

The legacy you leave, which I call your vapor trail, is always about how others remember you. No, don't live your life as a popularity contest trying to gain everyone's love. Live your life as consciously as possible in service to your passion that will create an amazing vapor trail.

The more you work kindly with each of your myriad of relationships, the better off you will be, the better off your world will be. Kindness doesn't mean sweetness. It can be harsh when needed, but it comes from a soft heart. The Sufis say, "soft like wax, that warm gooey center of the candle when lit, that is your true heart space." How can we maintain a soft heart, especially when we get triggered? This tool is one of my favorite from my vast and powerful tool kit.

THE TOOL

I want to share one powerful tool I learned and use all the time to save me and my essence.

This breath is called Sitalie Breath or Calming Breath. It calms and connects you to your parasympathetic nervous system, which is the aspect of your nervous system which allows you to relax, calm down, receive and become more vast. It is the being aspect of you.

You can do this anytime and almost anywhere. If you practice this, it will be there for you when you need it because it will be in your memory bank.

To begin:

Lightly bite the tip of your tongue and inhale as slowly as possible through the sides or corners of your mouth. Exhale long and slow through your nose. As the breath cascades over your tongue and your saliva, it cools your parasympathetic nervous system and calms you down. Do this as a practice for three minutes. When feeling stressed, do this breathwork till you feel calmed down and past the danger zone of saying things you will regret.

Biting on your tongue keeps you from saying things you will regret. After saying things that flop unconsciously out of your mouth, it only feels good for a moment. I like to say it is like wetting your pants when you have had to go for a long time; it only feels good for a brief moment, then there is the long, arduous clean-up time, and it's never truly cleaned up, is it? So lightly bite your tongue and breathe with Sitalie Breath.

If you are here reading this, I trust you know that you want to leave a legacy that will leave this world, this universe, and this multiverse more whole, more loving. That is commendable, and you need support and good tools to create the habits that will sustain you in that mission.

I trust you will utilize the gifts encoded here, for we care about you and your legacy. It affects us all. We are on this journey together. We are now consciously connected, related, and in a relationship. Blessings

I look forward to connecting more in the days to come. Here is your link to collect your free gift. https://gurutej.com.

Gurutej Khalsa began studying with Yogi Bhajan in 1969.

Yogi Bhajan is credited with bringing Kundalini Yoga to the United States. As one of his original students, Gurutej emerged as a founding practitioner of Kundalini. Gurutej is considered a foremost authority on Kundalini Yoga and is internationally recognized as one of a handful of Kundalini Yoga Masters.

In 1972, Gurutej co-founded 3HO Canada and a series of Ashram and Kundalini yoga centers and businesses all over Canada for 17 years.

Co-founder of Golden Bridge Los Angeles in 2000. For years, she has led projects feeding the homeless in Los Angeles in the downtown area.

In Los Angeles, she taught yoga and meditation as a community service for 11 years; weekly at Hamilton High School, an inner-city racially-mixed school.

She has taught in India, all over Europe, South America, the US, and Canada.

For over 50 years, Gurutej has been teaching all over the world and is considered an authority on Kundalini Yoga/meditation/conscious lifestyle. Gurutej has been living her destiny and continues to awaken the spirit of all she touches. She is known as the Energy Guru. Her mission is to give everyone the tools and support to become their own Energy Guru.

As a prolific writer, Gurutej is an author of five popular books, including *A Slice of the Beloved: Connection for Relationships, The Moon She Rocks You: Revealing the Secrets of Women's Inner Emotions, The 13th Month: How to Get an Extra 29 Days Each Year, Empower Your Essence And the Art of Energy.* She has also developed the Empowered Energy Academy to support people's empowerment journeys.

She has worked with many businesses including, Michael Starr, Disney, Big Buddha Babba, Urgent Care Centers, Khalsa Mcbreaty Accounting, and many more.

Through her True Success program, a proven success system, she mentors people to reclaim their empowered energy in all areas of their lives, self, relationships, and work, using challenges to empower their energy and their lives. The outcome is you will have the energy you crave and feel connected and empowered in all aspects of your life.

When she is not traveling the world and teaching, Gurutej can be found at The Blessings Center in the Los Angeles area. You can find out more about how Gurutej can serve you to create the habits you need to be the amazingly empowered version of you at https://gurutej.com.

CHAPTER 3

TRANSFORMATION FOR GROWTH

BE THE TRUEST VERSION OF YOURSELF

Doreen Hillier, BA, BCC, Rev., DTM

Introduction

How often have you said you were feeling fine when underneath, your world was chaotic, and life was seemingly falling apart?

I've had many experiences where I smiled and pretended so I didn't burden someone else, until one day, someone looked me in the eye and said, "Doreen, it's okay to need help."

I was programmed to take on a lot of responsibility as a child while my mom was sick with kidney failure and my dad was away working on construction three weeks at a time. It was common for me to go to school, come home and scrub floors, cook dinner, look after my baby brother, and help be a little nurse to my mom.

Right out of high school, I left my small town in Central Newfoundland and went to the big city of Toronto. The lights as the plane landed looked like dancing, sparkling diamonds. I stayed at an apartment with a couple of girls from church, and my boyfriend only lived about three buildings away. I landed a job at an insurance company typing fire sprinkler reports.

At 18, I married and had two children. Many times I faced the hands of an abusive husband. Nine years after my marriage, at 10:30 am, I ran from my Bramalea home into the rain covered in blood and beer. My children, age five and seven, ran into the street behind me. The last sound

I heard as I ran out was the knife drawer opening. After this, I was told how my husband planned on taking my life. He was having an affair at work and chose another woman. I quickly learned that abuse is never to be tolerated—never. We never went back.

MY STORY

I started my healing journey from a horrible, abusive marriage at 27 years of age and focused on putting my children, health, and well-being as the main focus.

I joined Toastmasters as a very shy person and, in my icebreaker speech, I read every word of the four-to-six-minute speech, including my name. "Hello, my name is Doreen Hillier, and I thought I should know who I am at least." Afterward, I laughed, but I will never forget how I felt with my knees knocking and grasping the lectern and reading every word.

Practice and encouragement helped me grow into a confident speaker and leader. Taking on leadership roles was a learning and growing opportunity I wouldn't shy away from. Walking across the stage in 2016 and receiving the International Presidential Citation Award for upholding the Toastmasters Core Values was a proud moment. An even better moment was recognizing all the people who have impacted my life and all the lives I've impacted. So many became friends outside the organization.

I'm still a member of Toastmasters International and help on an advisory committee for the Club Growth Director of District 86.

Was it always clear sailing? No, of course not. There were times when I felt like I could not go on. I needed a boost of courage and a boost of encouragement to continue.

God called me to care for others, myself, and my children. It took a while for me to mature and grasp that wisdom.

I worked and returned to college and university, getting my Business Administration Diploma, BA, and major in accountancy. While being a single mom, working and studying, there were times I just wanted a shoulder to lay my head on, to know everything was going to be okay. I opened and ran my accounting firm with over 200 clients, worked long hours, and instilled in my children to do well in school. I searched many inspirational books that said children could not retain information if they came from a single-parent home. I was determined to overcome all odds and obstacles. I can proudly say my children graduated grade 12 on the principal's honor list. Both are married and have great careers, and their spouses have great jobs as well. I have two grandsons, one seven and one five years of age.

While helping 200 clients in my tax accounting firm and working long hours, I felt a call from God saying he was taking me in a different direction. This is where trust comes in, big time. God was going to use me in speaking, writing, and leadership. I led Toastmasters District 86 with a team of 4500 members to distinguished status, did hundreds of speeches, and joined the Public Speakers Association and Public Speaker's Guild.

Are you listening? God asked me to slow down. He asked me to listen so that I could hear opportunity knocking. At first, I rebelled. I didn't obey, and I didn't listen.

I got an epiphany—an awakening—an understanding of the words:

Love others as you love yourself.

I realized I hadn't truly loved myself and looked outside myself for love and validation.

As I listened effectively to guidelines and followed expert advice, the puzzle started to form and began fitting into pieces. Things started to flow. I said yes to opportunities more often.

I said yes. In Seoul, South Korea, I had the opportunity to speak at the university and teach/guide students in presentation skills as 30 percent of their final marks hinged on doing a presentation. The stakes were great. We had to do tongue twisters. Getting into the presentation skills, I taught them vocal variety, effective pauses, and a good opening, body, and conclusion. I asked them to say my name, Doreen. It sounded more like Doween. So with the tongue twisters and pronunciation of the "r" (rice, not "l" lice) and practicing, they were able to get it. I used an analogy of a young boy who sees his horse across the field and knows it's thirsty. He walks across the field, ties a rope around the neck, and leads the horse to the water, but the horse does not drink. So it is. "I can teach you the skills you need to do the presentation, but it's in the application of those skills that you'll present and get your top marks." I was thrilled to learn that all 72 tried to apply, and some did get 30 out of 30 on their presentation. The director of the university took me to lunch and gave me a wonderful letter of recommendation. I'm that same person who read every word of her icebreaker speech, including her name. You can see that when we apply, practice good habits, learn, and practice some more, we make a difference in our own lives and others.'

With my clients, I learned there would be obstacles, but if you keep your eye on your goal, you'll find a way to jump over or walk through the obstacles to have what you desire.

What makes your heart and soul burn with passion? Mine is helping others. I was born to care.

In 2017 I received my Pastor's license, did chaplaincy work in a hospital. I loved helping others. The passion was burning in my heart. Here I was 40 years later, following my true calling to love myself and love others, bringing out the best in others, and being the truest version of myself.

After studying organizational behavior, cognitive behavior therapy, solution-focused therapy, chaplaincy, and biblical counseling, I learned which questions to ask my clients to help them discover and unlock their potential.

TFG, which stood for Tax and Financial Accounting, was reborn to TFG: Transformation for Growth.

Now I know that loving myself would be like loving others with no assumptions, barriers, race preferences, cultural differences, or gender differences—to love as God loves. Giving everyone the permission to just be, breathe, and walk alongside them, giving them hope and encouragement.

Each person is different and unique. Each person has gifts and wisdom inside themselves. That is why we talk, listen, and dig deeper as joy and happiness comes from within.

I decided to put together (develop) a course curriculum called Women on Their Own, whether single, divorced, or widowed. It was mainly about budgeting and the habits/triggers that women have when it comes to purchasing things. One woman who registered asked, "I'm married. Is it okay to come to your course?" She said, "I witnessed what my sister-in-law went through when her husband passed. She was lost on how to pay bills or budget." She, Mary, wanted to take my course and be prepared in the event that her husband passed before her. What I didn't know is about six weeks (ten hours) into the course is that we would learn something other than what I had prepared for. Mary brought a couple of poems to class that had nothing to do with the course and gave them to me to read. She loved writing poetry. She said that her professor in college and her family laughed at her. What I read was good.

I offered to edit 100 of her best poems and put her in touch with a publisher. *Keeper of Memories* by Mary Chabot, a book about her family, was published. I remember going to her house while she was receiving purchase orders for her books and looking in her eye and saying, "Mary, you are now a 72-year-old lady in business for yourself." I opened my copy of her book and saw that she had given me credit as editor. Mary's eyes sparkled like diamonds. She was so excited to finally have her dream come true. About four years ago, Mary passed, but her family wrote about the legacy and poetry book she left, *Keeper of Memories in her obituary.*

Remember I said opportunity knocks? While I was helping Mary get her poems published, a poetry contest came into my inbox. My first instinct was to give it to Mary, but I decided to let her focus on getting her book written and published. Instead, I wrote a poem about my mom—my best friend and confidante. I called it Divine Intervention. I won the International Published Poetry contest and received a 24 karat gold William Shakespeare coin and a trophy.

This sparked me to write a book about my mother entitled *Sitting in My Mother's Chair*. It's about her faith and her unconditional love for me. Once I have put the finishing touches on it, it'll be published.

I gave hundreds of speeches, wrote books and articles, and found it took courage—lots of it—to release the words inside myself and expose them to the world. I am reminded that we all have gifts or talents. As the chorus I learned in Sunday school says, "Hide it under the bushel—no, I am going to let it shine." I believe each one of us should let our light and love shine. Don't let doubt, worry, or insecurity hold you back from following your dreams and desires.

When experiencing conflict or naysayers, changing your mindset may help you. Here's a tool I used when I was in leadership at Toastmasters.

When people could not work together to get a job done, I asked them to use this analogy: think of him or her as sandpaper—rubbing you to refine you to be a better person. The following year a crowbar could not separate these two people as they worked well together. Growing pains are hard, but we transform when we grow.

We are God's children designed to live our dreams and fulfill our potential. TFG (Transformation For Growth) looks at the physical, emotional, mental, spiritual, financial, relaxation, fun, and travel aspects of a full life. We all have areas that will need to be addressed and reflected upon. It's a daily living, one day and step at a time, that we'll realize just how far we have come as we keep putting one foot in front of the other.

I'm in the process of also writing a book on leadership and presenting workshops on leadership. I learned that it isn't an easy job, just leading our own lives, but in the leadership journey, we're learning and growing and influencing others to grow, and I feel it's worth the effort. I did one workshop on leadership that had 72 attendees. One man and one woman followed up years later to say how it impacted their lives. The man was working for a company where he was bullied for 25 years, but something in that workshop caused him to shift his mindset, and he went home and talked with his wife. He quit his 25-year job and started a business of his own. He was so excited to tell me at our next conference what a difference it made in his life. The woman emailed me ten years after that particular workshop and asked, "Do you remember me?" She kept notes from that exact workshop and found they helped her when she lost her long-time employment. The notes helped her find hope and confidence to rise above the temporary situation. Her thanks and enthusiasm said it all.

I realized touching lives, caring for and inspiring others, and having an impact have fulfilled my true calling. In so doing, I'm helping myself and growing as well. I could say that the experience I joyfully receive from having a fan club that appreciates the positive messages and testimonials I post on Facebook makes me feel proud that I can assist in uplifting someone else's experience and be aligned with my true calling.

Joy and happiness come from within. We can choose, despite circumstances, to have joy, peace, and happiness. We have to take action toward that calling to make our dreams a reality. No matter the differences we encounter, they can work together in harmony with the right tools. In life, we all have ups and downs. It's usually in the valley that we learn the lessons, and on the mountain top, we get to reflect and enjoy what we've accomplished.

Covid tried to stop us and slow us down, and some of us have been impacted by the loss of health or loved ones. I lost my future husband to Covid on May 3, 2020, and the grief process was very hard. One thing he would have wanted me to do is continue living, giving back, and making a positive difference in this world. We need to appreciate every moment of our lives and always do the best we can with God's help.

Thank God for technology and the ability to meet Rochel and a couple of her friends and colleagues. We talked and connected, and here I'm experiencing a chapter in her book that I hope will touch the lives of everyone who reads it.

Life-long learning is a goal of mine, and I would love it if you would come on this journey with me. Let's grow and glow together.

THE TOOL

Do you journal?

- Every day take 15 minutes to yourself to write down your thoughts, experiences, and ideas into a journal.
- Sit down with a pen and notebook and let it flow from the heart. Sometimes it's healing; sometimes, it's enlightening. Date it so that you can reflect on it later.

Do you have a gratitude journal?

- Every day take 15 minutes at night to write down three things you're grateful for that day and make sure it's dated. Sometimes I feel there are more than three.

Some questions to get you pondering to help you come up with ideas of what to write might be as per the following:

Are you living your most passionate life? Write in the journal about it as if you were talking to your best friend.

Life becomes more fulfilling when you align with your true self. Write down all your goals, aspirations, wishes, and dreams. Watch as they unfold.

Do you have a community of support? Write about the people that touched your life that day.

Doreen Hillier, BA, BCC, DTM is a pastor/chaplain, businesswoman, author, speaker, award winner, mother of two, grandmother of two, and lives in Guelph, Ontario, Canada. Doreen loves working with and helping people realize their full potential. Her friends and family have given testimonials of Doreen's inspiring attributes and how she has touched their lives. Doreen is a woman of faith and walks the talk. She is trustworthy, caring, and compassionate. In her workshops and speaking, she inspires others to take the necessary steps to improve their lives. Doreen feels helping others inspires her to make this world a better place. She loves to share the love and light, and those who know her well know that her love and caring ways are genuine, and her love shines through with God's grace and compassion.

Gift:

I would like to offer an hour of counseling for free to the first 100 people who contact me. Please go on my website at www.tfgconsultinginc.com and make an appointment. Let's get on this journey of discovery to find the hidden treasures underneath. We can use Zoom, WhatsApp, or FaceTime live to communicate at a distance.

CHAPTER 4

THE UNSTOPPABLE DREAMER

HOW TO SUCCEED DESPITE ANY OBSTACLE
A STORY ABOUT IRENE VAKSBERG

Alexis Ybarra

MY STORY

Coming to America was a dream. The land of opportunity, hope, and a chance at a better life. In 1979, at just 11 years old my father, mother, sister, and I had to leave the Soviet Union. We left the Soviet Union due to Jewish persecution. The hope and dreams my family had for themselves wouldn't have been remotely possible if we stayed there. We had to wait in long lines for food rations, and times were tough for us out there. My father was luckily a well-connected and respected man in the community, so he was able to get necessities we might have needed at difficult moments. Even though my life started in a small town called Gomel, it was just the beginning of a long journey of survival, perseverance, and chasing the American dream.

When we came to the United States, the first place we resided in was Providence, Rhode Island. My parents always told me that this was the land of opportunity. If you want something, go and make it happen. We didn't know a word of the English language, and some of the ways we were able to pick it up was watching channel seven news with my father.

My mom and dad brought us to the land of opportunity where dreams could become a reality. I wanted to make my parents proud and follow the affirmations they gave me to go after the dream I wanted to accomplish, which was to become a hairdresser. But before I tell you that story of how I got my dream job, I need to tell you what I did before I got here.

I've always been an entrepreneur, just like my father. I was shy growing up, but as time went on, I came out of my shell when my confidence in the English language started to develop. My first job was at 12 years old, doing the paper route in Rhode Island. I was one of the paper route girls of the year in the area and received recognition for it, which made me feel special being the new girl in town. It was a big moment for me, and having this recognition made me feel proud of the work I was doing to help support my family. I also was a babysitter at 13 years old, cleaned homes, and worked with my parents at the swap meet selling sweaters. Work was what was needed of me and how I was able to support them in trying to get them to where they wanted to go.

When I saw my parents start their own business at the swap meets, it encouraged me to want to be my own boss. I knew at 11 years old that I wanted to be a hairdresser. My first client was my sister when I grabbed a pair of kitchen scissors and attempted to give her bangs. Safe to say that it was a lop-sided bob cut, but I knew at that moment that it was my destiny—shoutout to Central High School in Providence, Rhode Island, where I was a part of the vocational-technical school for hairdressing.

I graduated high school with a license in cosmetology/hairdressing. In 1987 I moved to sunny Los Angeles, California, in hopes of one day working for José Eber. I hustled my way through LA and got my first salon job at 19 years old. It was an exciting time for me, but I knew I needed to get more experience in the beauty industry before I walked into a famous hairdresser's salon.

After a few years being in Los Angeles, I met a boy, fell in love, and got married at 21 years old. I had a daughter and got divorced at 23 years old, now a single mother. I had a newborn and navigated my hairdressing career all at once. I was the first person in my immediate family to get divorced.

I probably still would've been married if it wasn't for my car accident. A drunk driver t-boned us and changed my life forever.

At times I feel like I'm a cat with nine lives. The accident that my barely year-old daughter and I got into while in the backseat required the jaws of life to get us out of the passenger seat. I was black and blue on one side of my body, and in the most excruciating pain I've ever been in. I had an out-of-body experience where I came face to face with God. I saw my life flash before my eyes, and God told me, "Your life isn't over yet. You need to stay on Earth for your daughter, and you will be the only person that can help her go through life." I was running through a field of flowers, but my reality on Earth felt like a war zone.

When I came back to life from that accident, I needed to make some changes in the way I lived, and who I shared my life with. I wasn't happy. I got divorced, and my family wasn't happy with that decision because of how the community would feel about it. But I chose myself over what people thought. After you meet God and come face to face with death, you need to make choices in life that can be difficult but necessary for a better life.

Then I moved to a new salon in Beverly Hills where a beautiful family embraced me with open arms. I was still in the process of divorcing my first husband and setting boundaries with my mother. She didn't allow me the space to be myself. My oldest daughter wasn't the easiest child to raise because of her mental and emotional health. It was hard being a single mother, balancing a career, and going through the emotions of everything the car accident brought to the surface in my life.

I got married again at 29, and then we had my beautiful second daughter at 31. We tried for another, and I had a miscarriage at 34. At this time, I had created my American dream of opening my own hair salon at 33 years old. It was the most incredible moment in my life to see my last name in lights. It was such a powerful moment to show my parents that all the sacrifices they had made coming to America weren't wasted.

In spite of all the wonderful achievements happening in my life from the outside, it was all falling apart on the inside. I was constantly working and barely getting a second to catch my breath. My oldest daughter was going through so much emotional stress and trauma during this time. I felt hopeless, and had no way to help her heal from her past. I was having trouble in my marriage and, on top of that, mourning my miscarriage. I was trying to find the silver lining in all the darkness that was taking over my life. I knew how important the hair salon was for me and that the little girl from the Soviet Union was trying to make her hairdressing dreams a reality.

I was involved with my community and collaborated with local artists to showcase their art on my walls. We then donated my cut of the profits to a charity of the artist's choice. I worked with women's groups and donated food and haircuts to those in need. My salon felt like a community center where I wanted people to feel at home. The salon was my safe place and where I felt like I could do what made me happy. I ended up getting divorced again and moved on to a new chapter in my life.

Fast forward to a life-altering moment; my 43rd birthday. I thought at this point that everything was going well. I had amazing friendships and was going after my passion, but it all came to a crashing halt on the way to a restaurant with my friends. A man fell asleep behind the wheel and t-boned the passenger side of the car. I spent my 43rd birthday in an emergency room, not knowing at the time the severity and long-term impact of my injuries.

This car accident took my hair salon business away from me and was the cause of lost friendships and my will to live in the process. The pain was my everyday reality, and I had no hope for a future without pain medication for five years of my life. I was in chronic pain, major depression, PTSD and experienced shaking spasms as a result of the trauma caused to my body. Doctors gave me no answers or hope, and made me feel like I was the problem. They put me on opioids and pain killers, which just numbed the pain temporarily. It was a temporary fix for a long-term issue.

Epidurals and hip injections were the only things able to keep me on my feet without shaking. My body deteriorated every time I went through those procedures, but they were my only option at the time.

I was angry with the universe and God for allowing this to happen to me again. I felt like everything I loved and enjoyed at one point in my life was taken away from me instantly. At some points, I contemplated taking my own life. I felt like I was given no other options, but I knew I had to live for my daughters and family. I felt trapped in my own body. The pain, endless hospitals, prescriptions, and the sacrifice of my daughter taking care of me made me feel hopeless for five years.

This was my second major car accident, and in some ways looking back at it was a wake-up call. I wasn't surrounding myself with true friends or living my mission. I was stuck in a reality that wasn't my journey anymore. God sent me into a crash, and it was the hole I needed to crawl out of in order to become the person I am today.

One of my customers that has been a big supporter throughout my whole car accident journey reminded me of a phrase I used to tell her when she was in my chair—words I now live by daily. She reminded me of the affirmations I once told her, "Giving up was not an option, baby steps are better than no steps, and this is just a moment." I kept praying for a miracle and wanted to find a natural solution to my chronic pain and shaking spasms. I asked God, "Show me a sign and send me a miracle for something to stop this pain and give me a new purpose in life."

In 2017 my close friend found a drug-free, non-invasive neurological wearable technology sock that changed my life. Within seven seconds, I stopped shaking. I finally came out of the darkness I was in for so long and felt that I had hope and something to hold on to. But at that moment, I didn't know I had a purpose attached to my new mission in life. It was a miracle I never thought would come. It came with so much more. I thought finding the product was the end, but it was just the start of my journey.

My faith was restored when my miracle came to me in an unexpected way. God was amazing when he answered my prayer. I had hope for a future again. I could now walk again and do things I couldn't do before. I started sharing my story on Facebook Live and TikTok. People started following my journey. I've been able to find joy in helping people live drug-free and pain-free lives. This neurological wearable technology is my mission, passion, and hope when I didn't have those things. This brings a smile to my face every day, and I wake up feeling a new sense of purpose in my life now.

My mission is to show people that miracles exist and come in ways we least expect them. Hold on to hope and accept the gifts people want to give you. Chronic pain felt like my life sentence. Now I want to inspire people to live their life to the fullest and continue to bless people with better quality of life each day I can.

THE TOOL

The actions I took to recover from the pain of my second car accident were adjusting my diet, wearing neurological wearable technology products, hiking, and dancing. Food is such a big part of my life. I loved going to restaurants before my second car accident and trying different kinds of foods from all over the world. I started to juice more consistently once I found NWT because I could finally think clearer and not worry about the pain but instead focus on my internal body functions. I was eating a pescatarian and vegan diet for about four years after finding this product. In those four years, I felt the best I have felt in my entire life!

Another part of my action plan was to be open to new products that help with pain management and recovery. If it wasn't for my friend being so persistent about trying this product, I don't know where I would be today without it. This NWT changed my life for the better and those around me. It's about being consistent with it; it takes discipline and hard work, just like anything.

Going on hikes was my favorite pastime before my second car accident. I loved being around nature. The strength and power I felt climbing up that hill felt so rewarding. Now that I am able to hike again with this product on, I feel like I have a major part of my life back. I've met so many amazing people on my hiking trail and started a series on my Facebook live when I hike all the way at the top of the hill, telling people about my journey from where I used to be to now.

That is the same way I feel about dancing. I remember at one point feeling like I wouldn't be able to dance again. Now, every Friday, I post dancing videos on TikTok/Facebook and tell people not to give up on themselves. Dancing brings me joy and is a way I can express myself in a fun way. I encourage whoever reads this to find hobbies that bring you joy and implement them into your daily activities. If it wasn't for all these things that I have done in different phases of my life and in my healing journey, I don't know where I would be today.

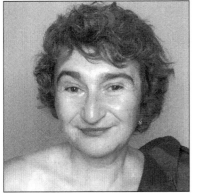

Irene Vaksberg, hairdresser for 38+ years, based in Los Angeles and Independent Associate of Got Health Neurological Wearable Technology, is on the mission to change lives. Her mission is to inspire people from all walks of life. She is currently on the mission to help people get a better quality of life using drug-free, non-invasive neurological wearable technology products.

Irene shares her story about her car accident journey on Facebook and Instagram live daily, telling people about her long battles with chronic pain and how she found hope in the end. She advocates for a positive mindset works with non-profit organizations, and hopes to one day open a women's center for at-risk youth with mental health issues.

Irene has two daughters, four grandchildren, and a dog named Emma. Without the support of her daughter, she wouldn't have been able to publish this book chapter, so she appreciates her contributions to the making of this story about her mother's inspiring life.

If you want to connect with Irene, reach out to her on the attached platforms.

Irene Vaksberg - Got Health

Email: ivaksberg.business@gmail.com

Independent Voxxlife Associate

Website: gothealth.voxxlife.com

Instagram: gothealth_vaksberg

LinkedIn: https://www.linkedin.com/in/irenevaksberg

Youtube:https://www.youtube.com/channel/ UC4w02IDaV0QEw36w7V1nfhQ

Facebook: https://www.facebook.com/irene.vaksberg

Tik Tok: irenevaksberg

CHAPTER 5

GROWING YOUR CONFIDENCE

CRITICAL STEPS TO LEADING IN THE 21ST CENTURY

Vicki Noethling, DTM

MY STORY

I am one of seven kids and the second to the oldest. Being the second in line meant that I received a lot of life lessons early on, and, as you can imagine, this made me somewhat of an old soul. Mothers stayed home to raise the kids, and dads went out to bring home the paycheck. My mother was a talented artist and married my dad at 19 on December 26th. They moved from a small town in western Pennsylvania to Dover, Delaware, where my father enlisted in the army. They were back in Western Pennsylvania the following year with a baby born the day before Christmas. Thirteen months later, I was born. Scientists tell us that our early childhood imprints on us the behaviors that will shape our lives. That must be true because my first experience of conflict and the feeling of fitting in was when my sister realized I took her crib and proceeded to climb in and sit on me. The relationship between us carried on that way for many years. Growing up, I had low self-esteem. Not smart enough. Not athletic enough. Not pretty enough. Nicknamed Vic the Stick, I was tall and thin. Some of you might think that is great, but believe me, it's not always good. However, this instilled in me the constant desire to work harder, read and learn more, and pursue self-development wherever I could.

In high school, things began to change. I changed by expanding my network of friends, pushing myself to go outside my comfort zone. The more I tried, the better things became. Then at some point late in my sophomore year, I realized college was not in the cards for me financially. So, I changed my focus to business and began another shift in my life. I began to pursue what I wanted and not what I thought others wanted for me. Have you ever found yourself doing that? I didn't even have the pressures of social media. Today, we have to shut out the noise and reach deep down to find the courage to know that who we are is good enough.

Fast forward, graduating in the top ten of my class and finishing business school in six months, I began working for an accounting firm. That's where I learned my first management technique. That was when I was told, "You're doing great," but there was always a fill in the blank. "You did a great job here, but you didn't quite meet our needs with that report." There was that "but" keeping me from being proud of my accomplishments. Once again, I saw myself as limited and lacking confidence. Now I could apply that management technique here. Sure, my lack of college might hold me back, but I could use that love of learning and self-development to change my circumstances. Perhaps you were one of those Franklin Covey users or some other sort of planner. I can remember having cassette tapes in my car to listen to on the way to and from work. That is when things started to change again. At 21, I was married. At 27, I moved to Atlanta, and at 30, I became a new mom who worked as a construction coordinator. Then at 33, I began working for the CIO of UPS, and his mentorship changed my life forever. His ability to speak and teach inspired me to be more. More creative, more courageous, and more inspirational to my team. To trust in my gut and lead from my heart. When he retired, I felt the loss of a good friend and mentor and turned to self-development again to keep the right mindset for success.

Have you ever met someone like that? Thinking back, I probably had several individuals who guided me. You often don't realize it until you look in the rear-view mirror. He is who encouraged me to go into leadership. He challenged me and gave me the confidence to not give up. He also told me that if it's no longer fun, it's not worth you're doing it. He helped me find my courage. He helped me find my voice. I will be forever grateful to him.

DISCOVERING THE COURAGE WITHIN

Henry Kissinger once said, "A leader does not deserve the name unless he or she is willing to occasionally stand alone." Courage doesn't always mean taking on some battle. Think about when you wanted to do something but didn't because no one else would do it with you. You have what you believe is a great idea only to keep it to yourself because others will not see its merit.

Sometimes it requires courage to make that unpopular decision that'll enable you to realize your goals and potential. Howard Schultz, chairman and CEO of Starbucks, laid off 15,000 employees and shut down stores to save 180,000 employees. It took courage to do that, knowing the negative press it would generate. Months later, when the stock went up 2000%, it was apparent that his courage to make that unpopular decision resulted in a massive benefit for the employees and stockholders.

When interviewed and asked about a tough decision he had to make, President Bill Clinton said this. "If you have to make what you know is going to be an unpopular decision—make it quick. The longer you think about it, the more likely you will lose your courage to do the right thing versus the popular thing."

Often it's what's between our two ears keeping us from embracing our courage. Our imposter syndrome starts to create noise in our minds that slows us or even stops us from making the right decision. If you don't act quickly, you'll crumble under the stress and pressure of that indecision. Learn to trust your gut.

Tools to help with tough decisions - ask yourself these three questions:

1. When did you have to make a tough decision, and did things work out well?

2. When did you not go through with making the tough decision, and did the results not go well?

3. What challenging and perhaps unpopular decision should you be making right now but are putting off making that decision?

Think about your home life and professional life when pondering the above questions. That project is not going well. That relationship is toxic and keeps you from becoming someone you could be. Maya Angelou describes courage in this way. "Courage is the most important of the virtues because, without courage, you can't practice any other virtue consistently. You can practice any virtue erratically but nothing consistently without courage."

Whether or not you have courage is a personal choice. We can realize our potential only by our choices in life. Courage is a skill that we develop through aggressive practice and focus. It is not the absence of fear. It is the ability to act in the presence of fear. The journey to courage begins with the number one quality we all can possess – confidence.

GROWING YOUR CONFIDENCE

It's not your background, family, education, or experience that will predict whether you become tremendous and thriving in the 21st Century. Both Elon Musk of Tesla and Richard Branson dropped out of school. Despite this, they've risen to be a couple of the most wealthy and influential people in our time.

Confidence is the most powerful influencer in society, business, teams, and even the stock market. Think of George Washington, Martin Luther King, Jesus Christ, Winston Churchill, and Abraham Lincoln. They all shared the quality of confidence, which resulted in a tremendous impact on our history. What was the common denominator with all of them? It was their confidence and belief in themselves.

Even leaders in history that did not positively impact society, like Hitler, Osama Bin Laden, possessed the quality of confidence.

"People are looking for people who know what they are talking about to tell them what to do." A.L. Williams

You see this on the web and social media all the time. Even in the office, an employee continually asks their manager for the solution. They may think they're doing it because it's easy or quick, but perhaps the real reason is they lack confidence in their ideas. Certainty is a necessary element in our lives. People want others to tell them what to eat, what to watch, and what to do, and do so with grounded, passionate certainty. Go back to the day the Twin Towers were attacked. That day was devastating for our country. President George Bush climbed on a pile of rubble to address the crowd and demonstrated how a leader leads with confidence. He showed empathy. President Bush restored our faith. Then he put us back on track for the future. That small act, a moment in time, boosted his popularity rate to 79%. A confident leader can take a group from a moment of despair to a moment of greatness. A leader must be able to be calm in the storm. They must take responsibility and control, resulting in their ability to move us on to attack the problem.

Confidence provides that safety net for our family and our teams. Coach Mike Krzyzewski said it best, "A leader shows the face his team needs to see." When the world seems to be crashing in on you, what face are you showing? Your mindset, attitude, and mood will spread through your team. If you feel fear, it will spread like wildfire. Fear is due to your lack of confidence. It's up to you to build your confidence and overcome the past, deep-rooted practice imprinted from childhood that keeps you from reaching your potential.

THE TOOL

1. Are you showing the face your team needs to see?

2. Are you instilling confidence—being persuasive and influential?

3. How can you show up better?

Confidence plus the unique skills you bring to the table can propel you in everything you do. It is the single most attribute for high performance and is the exception. It motivates. It determines if we will fulfill our potential, our dreams. Confidence is the power to attract and influence. Being confident is not arrogance but natural and cannot be faked. Confidence is something we earn as it develops and cultivates. Based on prior experience and evidence, that grows as you journey through life.

We are constantly communicating, and the signal that attracts us the most is our confidence. It also is an attribute that attracts our future partners. It intrigues and helps us feel safe. We are comfortable in our skin, and that sense of ease is appealing. Because most of us lack self-esteem, we seek confidence in others. We follow people who believe in themselves because we feel they will succeed, and we want them to protect us.

Answer these questions:

1. Should you fake it til you make it?

2. Do you feel you lack confidence? First, admit it, and then look at six influencers that built your confidence.

3. Think about your childhood.

   a. What did you learn from your parents and family that impacts how you feel about yourself?

   b. How did your school experiences shape your confidence and self-esteem?

   c. What impact did those social settings have on you and your confidence?

   d. Now consider your work environment. Have any situations lowered your self-esteem and confidence?

   e. The media constantly is bombarding us with advertising designed to shake your confidence. It points out the gaps where you are and where you should be. It eats up your confidence by contrasting and comparing you to others. How does social media influence you?

   f. Religion also can impact our confidence levels. Have you been affected by your religious teachings that resulted in a feeling of lower self-esteem?

   g. Previous performance is one that often gets us. We tried it. It didn't go so well, so that's it. We won't do that again. It could have happened in our youth, high school, college, or even last week. It still makes an impression and can keep us from seeing a solution or reaching our goal because we lack confidence that we will do it better the next time. It is a good thing we didn't realize this when we took our first step, or there would be a lot of crawling adults around the world.

All these things shape your confidence. The good news is that you can rewire your brain at any age. You can reclaim your self-esteem. Your past does not have to direct your future.

TAKING ACTION IS THE ONLY WAY TO GET AHEAD

It's true. If you never act, you never progress from where you are today. Even a step that fails is outside of where you are today. You may be thinking you're afraid that what you do next may be no better than where you are today. But what if it's not? What if it's magical and fulfilling? What if it helps you and your family to a better life? Aren't you worth it? Don't you deserve it? In my anti-aging business, our CEO Jeff Olsen always tells the new people, "I will believe in you until you believe in yourself." That's what I'm telling you now. I will believe in you. Believe that you have the courage. Believe that you have the empathy and integrity to become that great leader. Confident and beautiful inside and out. I will believe in you until you believe in yourself.

I invite you to connect with me to help you navigate your journey to find your leadership confidence. Take a moment and answer these questions:

1. What are some simple steps to grow my confidence?

2. How can I get over my fear of speaking in public?

3. What do I need to do differently to be a more effective leader today?

4. What are five steps I can take to get my message heard?

5. What are the top three things keeping you from reaching your leadership goals?

Take those first steps, listen to your gut, and lead with empathy, integrity, and trust. Know that you are good enough and that your story is one we need to hear.

 **Vicki Noethling** is a distinguished toastmaster, speaker, trainer, coach, and certified project manager. Her primary focus is on helping other entrepreneurs effectively share their message in person and online utilizing simple speaking skills and techniques. With this, your confidence will grow, and you will be ready to take on the challenges and opportunities of a leader in the 21st Century. Originally from Trafford, Pennsylvania, Vicki now lives in Roswell, Georgia, with her husband, Bob. She has two daughters and two grandsons. She retired from UPS as a project manager in 2018 and has helped women and men look better, feel better and live better since 2016 with her anti-aging, wellness, and weight management products. She has been a Toastmaster for 24 years and has held many leadership positions with Toastmasters as well as with UPS. She launched her speaking, coaching career in 2021 and will be launching her podcast in 2022.

To connect with Vicki, visit her podcast - **The Find your Leadership Confidence Podcast** or visit my website at https://www.findyourleadershipconfidence.com.

Business phone number: 770-464-5414

Want to delve more into developing your confidence, leadership, and speaking skills? Here are two courses that might interest you:

Capture, Connect, and Commit:

https://courses.vickinoethling.com/manage/courses/1535136

Becoming a Confident Speaker:

https://courses.vickinoethling.com/manage/courses/1458983

You are welcome to join her free Facebook group:

https://www.facebook.com/Growing-Your-Confidence-112234791113215

CHAPTER 6

CANCELING CANCER

A ROOT CAUSE SOLUTION FOR HOLISTIC RECOVERY

Trina Hammack CHC, FDN-P

MY STORY

It was the most terrifying day of my life. The words, "You have stage four ovarian cancer," rang in my ears as the room spun and swallowed me up. My mouth went dry, I could hardly breathe, and I felt like *Alice in Wonderland* falling backward down a deep, dark, terrifying hole.

As I lay paralyzed on the exam table, visions of an old-fashioned wooden coffin played in my head. At the same time, my gynecologist droned on about my deadly condition. His words were a confusing jumble, tumbling out of his mouth, and the news blindsided me.

I kept thinking I was in some bizarre nightmare, and I'd wake up at any moment. *How could this be happening to me? After all, I'm a healthy, holistic practitioner living on the pristine Big Sur coast of California. Weren't cancer diagnoses reserved for those who abused their bodies with cigarettes, alcohol, and processed junk food? It made no sense how a healthy person like me could be receiving this horrific news.*

Even though cancer ran in my family, I never considered this my fate. My mother died of breast cancer treatment when she was 48 years old, and my grandmother, Trina, died of ovarian cancer at 36. And now, here I sat, stunned, facing the worst news of my life.

Over the next few months, the fatigue deepened as my belly continued to swell. My most overwhelming concern was for my nine-year-old son. I could not fathom leaving him motherless. I had to figure out a way to come to grips with this horrific and deadly news.

One day during an acupuncture treatment, my therapist offered some soothing words to my troubled soul. He said, "What if one day your son's life were threatened, and you could only save him from the other side? What if you had to die and leave your body to save his life?" That whole concept shook me to my core, and in a flash, I said, "If that were the only way to save him, then I would give up my life in a heartbeat."

In an instant, I resolved my inner survival conflict. As soon as I made that declaration, I also declared, "But I'm not dying! I am *not* leaving my son!" My conviction was so firm that wild horses could not have taken me from this world. I knew I needed to surrender so I could move forward. Even though I was still petrified, I found the courage to call the gynecological oncologist.

Without a biopsy, my new doctor wasn't convinced that the melon-sized mass was cancerous, and the only way to know was to remove it surgically. As terrifying as it was, I knew it was time to take the next step and have the surgery.

As if this journey weren't wild enough, things got even crazier. As we drove to the hospital for my surgery, the weather turned from sunny and bright to ominous and eerie. Dark clouds brewed, and lightning bolts crashed down from the sky, igniting the eucalyptus trees in our wake. I couldn't help but think this was some horrible omen. Little did we know that one of the most significant fires in California history had begun, and it would impact our lives for months to come.

As the fires raged around us, we narrowly slipped through the road closures to safely arrive at the hospital, where I was prepped for surgery. A sense of calm engulfed me, and I felt loved and supported by my family, both seen and unseen.

The surgery went smoothly, and as I opened my eyes in the recovery room, I saw the most beautiful woman standing by my bedside. I recall saying, "Are you an angel?" She smiled and said, "No, it's me, Daya." Magically, my dear friend, Daya, found her way to my bedside in the recovery room, which gave me the most reassuring sense of peace. Intuitively, I felt everything was going to be all right.

Once in my hospital room, I started all my holistic treatments with the love and support of my closest friends and family around me. Everything was calm until the next day when we received news that Big Sur was also on fire.

It was a beautiful, sunny day when, out of nowhere, a single black cloud rolled into Big Sur and shot a lightning bolt from the sky, torching the trees a mile from our home. When fires occur in rugged and remote Big Sur, they move extremely fast and are devastating. My friends and family sprang into action and raced down the coast to try and save our homes, leaving me alone in my hospital bed. Over the following months, the Basin Complex Fire continued to rage and became California's second-largest wildfire.

Due to the fires, I couldn't go home and heal in my sacred Big Sur, so I needed a plan B for my recovery. Once again, I found myself Divinely supported. My best friend, Janine, and her husband, Jose, were about to depart on a five-week trip to Peru and needed someone to care for their horses, desert tortoise, and a plethora of other critters. It was the perfect plan B!

Once I was discharged from the hospital, we settled into our beautiful new surroundings in the Santa Cruz mountains. Ten days post-surgery, Janine and Jose insisted on showing me their hiking route through the mountains to continue an exercise routine as I healed. As medical doctors, they knew it was vital to keep moving, so I painstakingly followed them along their rugged, three-and-a-half-mile hiking route. It was one of the most strenuous hikes I've ever done, but I survived!

For the next five weeks, my dogs and I hiked that trail every single day. My inner and outer strength grew with every step, and the fear of cancer retreated.

I'm not even sure how the next part happened, although I'm convinced my entire journey was Divinely orchestrated. I could feel the spiritual support as everything magically fell into place.

The two burning questions haunting me daily were:

1. *How could this happen to me?*

2. *Is ovarian cancer coming back?*

My doctors pressed me to do chemotherapy even though I knew it was not my path. After all, I watched my young and vibrant mother die from the effects of chemo and radiation, and I knew my fate would be the same. I had to figure out another way.

That's when German New Medicine (GNM) walked into my life. As a holistic practitioner, I knew a little about Dr. Hamer's German New Medicine work, although not enough to understand how it connected to my cancer diagnosis.

Dr. Hamer hypothesized that emotional trauma was the seed of all cancer and other diseases. He tested his theory with 40,000 cancer patients using CT imagery scans. Dr. Hamer found a correlation between emotional shocks and specific types of cancer. In addition, he discovered trauma marks on the brain scans of his patients, which tied to the cancerous organs. He could even tell if the cancer was complete or not from the brain scan.

Dr. Hamer's work fascinated me. As I dove into GNM classes, I learned how healthy people end up with cancer diagnoses. I was elated to have my questions finally answered, and I even had my own CT brain scan done. When my teacher read my CT scan and said, "Congratulations! It's not coming back," I was stunned and relieved, and at the same time, knew I had much to learn.

Dr. Hamer discovered that all liver cancer patients had survival conflicts and all ovarian cancer patients had loss conflicts. Breast cancer patients either had someone torn from their breast or had a home/nest conflict.

That theory certainly fit my mother's story and her breast cancer diagnosis. She had been in a massive battle over the house during her divorce from my stepfather, and that conflict was the seed to her breast cancer. With this nest/house conflict in mind, I realized I could've been setting myself up for breast cancer while the wildfires were threatening our home. Thankfully, I only held onto that trauma for a few weeks, and once our home was safe, my brain resolved the trauma, and my body dodged the breast cancer bullet.

At this point, you may be wondering how this trauma and healing process works. According to Dr. Hamer's work, there are three phases to any disease, the conflict phase, the resolution phase, and the healing phase.

The conflict phase begins when the person viscerally experiences an emotional shock or trauma. The longer the person holds onto this trauma without resolving it, the more their body breaks down tissue or builds a benign or malignant mass.

According to GNM, the emotional seed to ovarian cancer is a profound loss conflict, which makes perfect sense in my case. When I was three years old, I was abruptly taken away from my father in the middle of the night. Even though I don't remember the trauma, my brain recorded the incident. Being only three years old, I had no resources to resolve this loss, so my brain continued to store it until I met my father 43 years later. That's when I graduated from the conflict phase to the resolution phase.

During the resolution phase, the brain senses that the trauma has been resolved, and it's time for the body to heal. Upon resolution, Mother Nature takes over and sends a flood of amino acids to wash over the area of the brain holding the trauma. At the same time, a signal is sent to the organs to heal. If the trauma was intense and held for a long time, the healing could be so deep that it's cancer instead of a cyst.

When I met my father, subconsciously, my brain said, *she has her daddy back*, and in a flash, I resolved the deep, inner loss conflict I held for 43 years. I had no idea my brain settled this deep wound, but my body automatically knew what to do. It was finally time to heal my ovary that resembled a piece of Swiss cheese. As soon as my brain resolved the loss, I graduated into the third and final step, the healing phase.

During the healing phase, my right ovary began to swell. I became fatigued, and tentacle projections grew out of the ovary and entangled the organs in my abdomen. These tentacles searched for and absorbed nutrients to help heal my severely damaged ovary. The healing process for ovarian cancer lasts nine months, ironically, the same time it takes to create a baby.

The tentacles retract at a certain point in the healing process, and cancer dies from the inside out.

When the doctors biopsied the ovarian tumor, they found an aggressive stage 3 ovarian cancer already dying. This meant I'd made it through the entire healing phase, and I was going to live!

Our bodies naturally follow this three-phase process, whether we know it or not. It's pure biology. Instead of seeing yourself as sick when you get a cold or flu, ask yourself, "What did I just resolve to put me into a healing phase?" Don't worry; healing phases don't have to become cancer. A common cold, flu, or stomachache follows the same process.

With billions of microbes in our environment and bodies, why aren't we constantly sick? According to GNM, you are only susceptible to these microbes when in the healing phase. During the healing phase, microbes help *repair* the damaged tissue.

Honestly, I tried to disprove the GNM concept for two years until I realized that Dr. Hamer was right on the money. Every. Single. Time.

THE TOOL

You may be wondering, what can we do to empower ourselves and avoid horrific diseases? You'll be happy to know that there are many tools at our disposal to help us heal at the root cause level.

The main thing we can do is express ourselves and let it go! We call this exercise: *Name it. Claim it. Dump it.*

When you have a conflict with someone, express yourself and resolve it as soon as possible. The longer you hold onto it, the more damage you create inside your body. The sooner you speak your feelings, the faster and less severe your healing phase will be.

Remember, it doesn't have to be cancer when your body starts to heal. Instead, you could experience a stomachache or headache. Signs of a healing phase include fatigue, pain, inflammation, and fevers. Listen to and honor your body and get the rest that you need.

Even if the person you have the conflict with has passed on, you can still work through the issue. If the conflict happened when you were five years old, you'd need to express yourself as that five-year-old and not necessarily your current day self. Your adult self has an entirely different perspective than your child self, and it's usually your younger self that needs the expression. Your adult self can support your inner five-year-old by standing with them as they express themselves. This empowers and helps the inner child to let it go completely.

For this exercise, you'll need a photograph of the person you want to express yourself to. If the person has passed on, use a black and white photo and if they are still alive, use a color photo. Using their picture, talk, rant, rave, scream at it, or even draw all over the image. Would you please give your younger self the voice and expression they never had before? They have been holding onto this trauma for a long time, and they deserve a voice too. Say the things you never got to say. Don't filter yourself; go for it! Keep going until you feel peaceful, empty, and have nothing left to say.

Once you feel complete, take a step back and look at the person. They've heard you and understood you. Now ask them if they have anything they'd like to say to you. Many times, you'll be surprised at their response. They may even break into tears and ask for your forgiveness. If you can forgive them and release the pain, then you know that you have moved on. Holding onto anger, resentment, grudges, or any other negative emotion only rents space in your head and damages your body. Remember, holding on only hurts you emotionally and physically.

If you'd like to take your healing a step further, ask the person for the gift that this trauma holds for you. What is the silver lining to your whole experience? Getting to this point in your recovery releases even the deepest of pain, which can help you to feel lighter and happier. Gifts can come wrapped in packages that look like trauma. Sometimes we need to walk a rocky journey to find these once-in-a-lifetime gifts.

This process can help our children to be healthier and happier, too. Be sure to teach your children to speak up, resolve their conflicts, and find forgiveness as soon as possible. Let them have a voice, listen to them, and when they have entirely expressed themselves, they will naturally move on and not think twice about it. Once they've resolved their conflict, they may catch a cold. The next step is supporting their natural immune system with good nutrition and plenty of rest.

Many times, unresolved patterns of trauma seem to play out repeatedly in your life, like in the movie *Groundhog Day*. As these patterns repeat, your brain tries to solve the original conflict.

In addition to the Name it. Claim it. Dump it exercise; creating a timeline can help identify your original conflict patterns. The simple act of creating a timeline is a powerful therapy and can help your brain to realize that the traumas are over and it's time to heal.

To make a timeline, you'll need to know the age at which you became independent from your family. For example, if you moved out, had your job, and became independent when you were 20 years old, your brain will think in 20-year cycles. This means you'll draw your timeline with 20-year tracts.

Since you survived those initial years, your brain considers your past a successful program and will replay similar experiences during your life. Anything unresolved from the first years of your life will replay in the subsequent tracts on your timeline until your brain resolves the original trauma. Many times, just seeing the patterns on your timeline is enough to resolve the traumas and help you move forward in your healing journey.

I'd love to help you create your timeline, so I have included a video link to the timeline module from my Canceling Cancer program. This is a very empowering process, and I invite you to dive in more deeply. Once you see your patterns, your whole life starts to make sense. Here's the link to access Timeline Therapy: https://trinahammack.com/timeline-therapy/ Of course, if you need assistance with this process, feel free to reach out, and we can schedule some time to work together.

Even though it hasn't been smooth, I have been incredibly blessed and supported during my journey. Slowing down and listening to that still voice within has always been my saving grace. My silver lining along this journey has been twofold. My biggest blessings have been staying alive to raise my precious son and to be here to share this empowering message with you. I know that if you want to heal something for the last time, you must resolve the root cause.

Remember, we can't fight nature. Be bold. Be fierce. Be brave.

For over 27 years, **Trina Hammack** has been a noteworthy leader in the holistic health and wellness space. She teaches those who've lost hope how to ditch the band-aid approach and resolve their underlying Root Cause health issues once and for all.

Trina understands how it feels to be faced with a severe diagnosis. To completely heal from the life-threatening effects of Ovarian Cancer, Lyme Disease, Heavy Metal Poisoning, and Mold Toxicity, Trina knew she had to follow a natural approach. In doing so, she has made it her mission to help you empower yourself using natural methods.

Her clients call her *The Root Cause Warrior for Health* because she leaves no stone unturned when searching for a solution. Trina integrates state-of-the-art technology with ancient healing wisdom to create a unique healing path for each of her clients.

Trina has been featured in many summits including, The Truth About Cancer, Chronic Lyme Disease Summit, Parasite Summit, Depression & Anxiety Summit, Adrenal Solutions Summit, Healing with Vibration Summit, and more.

In her free time, you can find her indulging in sweaty spin classes, taking long walks on the beach, and enjoying the occasional romantic dinner with the love of her life.

CHAPTER 7

WAKE UP, TAKE CHARGE

PRIORITIZING DAILY INTENTION-SETTING TO MASTER LIFE

LJ Raspler, M.Ed.

MY STORY

It was September 2009. The H1N1 Swine Flu global pandemic was declared over a month earlier. My day began like any other except for a scheduled vaccination to combat the newest strain of influenza. I'd never considered getting a flu shot since good health had always been in my favor. With rising rates of Swine Flu, I figured, *What the hell?* Little did I know this decision would wind up compromising my well-being. That fateful day triggered my 12-year-long journey into a tunnel of pure, unadulterated darkness.

My incredible journey of Guillain-Barré syndrome, commonly referred to as GBS, was just the beginning. It was a bitter pill to swallow. Many people had never heard of it and even fewer could pronounce it. Guillain-Barré syndrome, spoken about now without shame (there I said it), sent my mind and heart reeling. This rare autoimmune disorder occurs after the immune system mistakenly attacks myelin sheaths, the insulators of healthy nerves, instead of a bacteria or virus in the body. Its victims suffer from debilitating nerve damage, oftentimes paralysis, and life-threatening breathing issues.

Despite the almost unshakeable denial, I sensed my body's nervous system going into a tailspin as symptoms began to rear their ugly head. I recalled a childhood friend's mother who had deteriorated rapidly due to developing GBS after taking the flu vaccine in the 70s. Sadly, she lost her battle. I was paralyzed by fear as my internet search led to a self-diagnosis that revealed I had developed GBS following the flu vaccine. My symptoms were indicative of a serious autoimmune response. *How was it possible that I, Laurie Raspler, queen of stability and reliability, could be whisked into such a life-altering state?* I rationalized and convinced myself that I was okay, which delayed my acceptance of the situation. As I learned, it's okay not to be okay.

My body (unbeknownst to me) was priming itself for the ultimate attack on my nervous system, the foundation for optimal functioning of all other organ systems. As my body slowly became taxed and stressed over time, chronic pain became the norm. Recurring viral and bacterial infections accompanied by antibiotics, as well as minor surgeries, weakened my body. This, combined with a concoction of ingredients contained in vaccines, left my body so vulnerable it gave way to my "dis-ease", inconveniences as I lovingly refer to them now. I experienced intense alarm at the onset of my initial symptoms within 24 hours after taking the vaccine. Like nails on a blackboard, tingling in my hands and feet drove me mad. My right arm felt odd, as did my feet. My tongue quickly took on a life of its own. The discomfort of its blanket-like, white coating paled in comparison to the offensive, metallic taste which rose upwards from my gut to my esophagus and persisted for months. Years later, a dental examination confirmed that the odd-shaped, white patches on my tongue, like states on a map, were symptoms of geographic tongue. My tongue, a roadmap going nowhere except to Hell, conjured up feelings of doom. A sensitivity to acidic and spicy foods lasted for 12 years. It became a family joke to eliminate lemon-laden foods when dining out because of my tongue's reactivity. Days were consumed with debilitating pain, numbness, tingling from head to toe (mostly in the extremities), achy, weakened muscles, brain fog, memory lapses, digestive issues, and utter exhaustion. As my symptoms intensified, nighttime became even more terrifying. I couldn't escape my overactive mind, caught up in the very gripping story unfolding before me. Sleep did little to alleviate the constant dread I felt. *Would tomorrow be a better day? Would this nightmare finally come to an end?* Its finale was unknown, yet hopelessness was never an option.

My emotional state, fraught with anxiety and panic, held me prisoner longer than I care to admit. I recall a particular day when I, attempting to spur my tired body on, went for a short walk. Barely making it around the block, I collapsed in my front yard. I was greatly relieved to have made it back and not been run over. That was all I needed! I continued to try to stay motivated, day after day, week after week, gingerly putting one foot in front of another, forging ahead. Certainly not a heroic deed, but more one of self-preservation. Not once did I ever think, *damn those invaders*, or *why me?* I dared not allow myself to fall prey to a victim mindset. I only wanted to be healthy, healed, and whole. Not much to ask for, right? As days, weeks, and months turned into years, I lived with chronic but manageable pain.

While my GBS symptoms consumed my body, mind, and spirit morning, noon, and night, I remained hesitant to seek medical intervention. Knowing how sick I was prohibited me from seeking the truth, and distrust further exacerbated my fears. I'd known something was terribly wrong as uncontrollable and irrational thoughts plagued my previously sound mind and buoyant spirit. A preoccupation with, *What the f***!* permeated my soul. My choices may appear crazy to some, but it's the path I chose, right or wrong.

Until this point, my entire life had always been predictable and perhaps mundane, but as my body was being ravaged, I couldn't help but want all the monotony and ordinary back. This realization shook the very ground I walked on, with silence as my protective shield against any further harm.

For the better part of my 60 years, I've always had a big voice that resonates loudly with all in earshot. Perhaps it was due to having a hard-of-hearing grandmother, a strong, over-protective father, or being the youngest of three. Wanting to be heard over others, my perception of my younger self is one that was seen and not heard. I sensed my big voice had been waiting, with patience, for the precise time to emerge to accomplish great things. As I've matured, I've seen the power of being heard, of being loud and proud.

The funny thing is, whenever I was sick, my voice was always the first thing to go. How ironic! My silence became louder than ever. I've unwaveringly continued to capitalize on a voice destined to be heard in spite of appearing defeated. As I fought with my inner demons brought on by GBS, I became too scared to talk about my health crisis. It wasn't until years later, as I opened up to learning the truth, that the factors which led to my illness were discovered. Like a ticking time bomb, after being silent for so long, I was ready to explode if I didn't take action. This reality became startling. From it came a profound realization; I'd become silenced by illness too damn long. It was time to regain my big, beautiful voice once again.

Confirmation can be liberating yet beyond humbling. While I went medically undiagnosed for more than seven years, my symptoms continued to lead me to believe I suffered from Guillain-Barré syndrome. Have you ever had that nagging feeling that you're right about something even though there's no concrete proof? I knew my avoidance of the medical community did nothing to affirm my condition. Consider it divine timing and gut intuition. In 2016, I sought out an allergist to determine what, if anything, had caused me to react so harshly to the Swine Flu vaccine years before. Bright red patches on my skin and a heightened tingling sensation shooting up my arms became apparent with testing.

The doctor casually told me, "Mrs. Raspler, it appears you have a sensitivity to thimerosal and heavy metals." Thimerosal is a mercury-containing compound used as a preservative in flu vaccines. "You had Guillain-Barré syndrome based on what you have described." It felt like I won the jackpot! I burst out joyfully as endless tears streamed down my face. I don't think I've ever laughed and cried at the same time. I received the long-awaited validation I craved. I was richer than ever, but I knew all the money in the world could never buy my health back.

Never once have I regretted my decision to be vaccinated and the path it led me down. The toll GBS took on my psyche was traumatizing, yet I've come out the other side a stronger and healthier me. I believe my path was always one of self-healing and self-love. Three years ago, I fully immersed myself in holistic health care practices as a means for healing. While I'm not a medical authority, I don't advise anyone to take my chosen path. However, seeking alternative methods invited hope and faith in my life. It was time to fully embrace my path to wellness. Through my ongoing journey with chiropractic care, acupuncture, Chinese medicine, Integrative Therapeutic Alignment (energy work), meditation, and yoga, I've discovered my true self. Immense gratitude fills my heart as I've found my purpose, with GBS as the catalyst for manifesting an abundant life I'm worthy and deserving of.

I still continuously manage triggers that arise. They say the journey is worth a thousand words, and after all these years, I've come to realize the power of this message. I often wonder why the awakening of the soul necessitates an event so mighty, like a thunderous roar coming down directly from the mountaintops shattering all illusions of reality. It was my seemingly mundane decision that altered the course of life as I knew it. Perhaps what transpired—the journey I've been on for the last 12 years— was exactly the "aha" moment I truly needed. I'm not saying we should all welcome and embrace being unwell, but as I confronted this nightmare head-on, I knew the only way to get real was to wake up and open my eyes.

I can say now with conviction that as I wake up and take charge each day, doors open. I've been hesitant to share my story all these years due to misconceptions surrounding vaccines and their potential risks. The truth has undoubtedly set me free. It takes guts to step into one's innate power, much like divine knowledge, as it leaps from the heart and glistens like a myriad of tiny moonbeams. My voice will never be silent again. I walk with my head held high as I eagerly and proudly share my truth. My path was always paved with gold. I only needed to open my eyes to see it.

THE TOOL

By sharing my compelling story, I'm hoping to help others on their journeys, whatever they may be. A very simple yet practical tool has assisted with my transformation: *prioritizing daily intention-setting to master life*. It has helped me manifest abundance and become the master of my own life.

Setbacks are the catalyst for inspiration! The only way out of darkness is to face it head-on, traversing its ugly tunnel to ultimately come out the other side into the light. I have gratefully welcomed daily intention-setting with an open mind and heart, like a gift tied up with a beautiful, red ribbon. I have altered my life using intention-setting as a tool, the driving force behind my GBS recovery.

Major changes necessitate a deliberate and well-orchestrated plan for life integration. As I began to live, eat, and breathe them in, my days became sunnier and brighter.

A 4-PART APPROACH

I want to provide an easy and simple routine to prioritize daily intention-setting to master life.

I implemented this routine two years ago. The routine is intended to be effective, methodical, and easy in its integration.

To derive optimal results, the 4-Part Approach must be included daily as part of your routine. I suggest using it with consistency and regularity as this will help maximize the best possible outcomes.

As you gratefully integrate daily intention-setting habits into your routine, you will become the captain of your ship and learn how to master life.

1. MEDITATION IS THE BEST MEDICINE!

As you move from sleep to the demands of daily tasks, the transition must flow easily and effortlessly.

Effective meditative practices are intended to clear out negative energy and increase vibrational energy. The meditation you incorporate should be flexible and feel-good.

Morning is the ideal time of day that allows you to be alone with your thoughts and consider what evokes vibrant well-being. Taking care of the most important person - yourself - sends a clear and distinct universal message as you prepare for a successful day ahead. *"What I want, wants me."*

Inviting in quiet, relaxing moments after awakening and certainly excluding any distractions from social media sets the stage for invoking positivity.

Meditation is best performed while sitting or lying down, with eyes shut in a relaxing space. Spiritual music or guided meditation may heighten your experience. To begin, take several slow, deep, energizing breaths to clear out negative energies and set your intentions. With each inhale, breathe in for a count of five, hold for three, and exhale to a count of five.

Allow your body and mind to surrender to the experience as you go deeper into your practice. Never rushed, meditation is intended to open you up to visualizing your intentions. If so desired, reciting affirmations, silently or aloud, can further assist by rewiring your subconscious. Upon completion of your meditation, remain still with your eyes closed for just a bit longer until you feel ready to slowly move your body once again. Now it's time to begin your day.

2. LET'S JUMP FOR JOURNALING

Journaling provides opportunities that are both cathartic and affirming. It can free the writer from the constructs that have prohibited living intentionally.

Never write purely for the sake of it. Even if you don't love writing, make journaling a fun and engaging experience.

Daily journaling can be used to liberate you from your fears, doubts, and limiting beliefs. It also promotes greater degrees of self-awareness.

Permit yourself to become a creative soul as you let your imagination soar. Include colorful pens and markers as a way of expressing emotions.

As you write each day, be sure to include worthwhile thoughts and/or quotes that inspire contemplation.

Compose messages of the day that inspire, express gratitude, include your top priorities of the day, or whatever else motivates you towards living a happier, more fulfilled life.

Be sure to add in positive affirmations to empower yourself with a healthier mindset that sparks hope and inspiration.

3. GIVE IN TO THE "G"

This step may be the most challenging to begin incorporating into your day-to-day routine, but it is perhaps the most gratifying. It allows you to live presently and fully in the moment as you pay close attention to your surroundings.

This "G" word is the only word you'll ever need. Without it, you have little.

Yes, I'm talking about GRATITUDE!

Gratitude can best be accounted for by recognizing, acknowledging, and appreciating what elicits joy.

Appreciation for all you have is fundamental to living a fulfilling and satisfying life.

Gratitude allows you to acknowledge your many blessings while attracting even more. As you express gratitude, you become happier and more optimistic about life.

Your life becomes more pleasurable, open, and expansive to endless goodness by expressing gratitude. It only takes a moment to express gratitude - it's that simple. Do it!

Stop. Pause. Look and listen to what's around as you take in your surroundings. Allow yourself to be fully present in that very moment. With a "life is happening for you, not to you" attitude, breathe in the goodness. No matter where you are, you'll begin to realize how much you have to be grateful for. Express, silently or aloud, what you're thankful for in that very moment. It's as if you've been sprinkled with pixie dust and there is beauty all around. Appreciate it. Feel it. Treasure it.

4. NEVER NEGLECT SELF-REFLECTION

This last step is critical for fueling greater momentum to living intentionally.

What you ultimately derive from your many experiences from intention-setting is yours alone to grow and learn from. You must remain mindful of those thoughts or actions that no longer serve you well.

It is beneficial to pay heed to necessary adjustments weekly, monthly, quarterly, or yearly. As both internal and external forces encourage minor shifts and changes, you always want to focus on what opens you up to a more rewarding life.

Your intentions necessitate patience and faith for your actions to align with your highest intentions. After all, don't you want what's best for yourself?

This completes A 4-Part Approach. Transformative, highly effective, and affirming.

Whatever moves your heart and soul to master life may be called in to serve as the foundation for creating a life you desire. The investment in yourself necessitates living intentionally as a means to claiming mastery over your own life.

I feel extremely fortunate to have created a no-frills, "can-do" routine for prioritizing daily intention-setting to master life. It is by no means an overnight solution that magically erases prior shortcomings or failings. The more I make intention-setting part of my day-to-day routine, life continues to improve. My health scare with GBS has inspired my winning attitude. Overcoming pain can bring forth joy! I've arrived at a beautiful place after 12 long years, and it feels amazing! Hear me loud and clear: *Wake up, take charge! Include prioritizing daily intention-setting to master life!*

LJ Raspler, born and raised in New York, currently resides in Virginia. She's an entrepreneur and fundraiser for veterans who draws upon her leadership skills, a prior career as a teacher, and creative flair. With her winning attitude, positive outlook, and boundless energy LJ is unstoppable in her mission to be of service. Never one to let challenges stand in her way, LJ began a committee in 2004, with support from her synagogue, to provide shelter and meals to homeless men even as the idea was met with resistance. She ran the committee until 2007, a year after she returned to college to study Spanish and ultimately obtained a Master's in Education at 50 years young. *As she wakes up, takes charge, and prioritizes daily intention-setting to master life*, LJ allows these to be the pillars for growth and fulfillment. Her most recent alliance with a VFW Post has gratefully opened up doors for LJ to begin the Cooking For Virginia Veterans program; with this, her dream to start a nonprofit serving veterans in need will soon be realized. In her spare time, LJ designs one-of-a-kind Beaded Blessings hanging charms to evoke powerful positivity in people's lives. In addition, LJ and her husband, Jesse, launched an e-commerce business specializing in creating Ethereal Escents Loose Smudge Herbs Kits to elicit positivity in one's home and life. Self-care rituals are a priority in her daily life. Other loves are spending time with Jesse and their kids, hiking, exploring new destinations, practicing yoga, cooking, and reading. Lastly, LJ loves animals of all kinds, including exotics that kept her children busy and entertained while growing up.

Facebook: https://www.facebook.com/lj.raspler

Victorious Veterans Fundraising:

https://victoriousveterans.voxxlife.com

Ethereal Escents: https://linktr.ee/ljraspler

CHAPTER 8

OWNING YOUR PURPOSE

SLAY YOUR HATERS AND RECLAIM YOUR DESTINY

JC Gardner

MY STORY

It was the early seventies in the South Bronx, a time where afros stood high, hoop earrings dangled freely, and platform shoes partnered with bell-bottom pants. In my world, a sliver of innocence still lingered, where we cooled off in fire hydrants, played hopscotch and double-dutch, and the flickering of the street lamps ushered us home. For the first twelve years of my life, this was my "hood," and it was in this setting, during a hot summer day while eating New York pizza, having a Coke, and a smile, I discovered my true purpose.

At the tender age of twelve, I had an amazing revelation. After exhausting all games imaginable, my best friend and I decided we should write stories. Thirty minutes later, my pages were filled, while hers were empty.

Writing was always easy for me, especially fiction since I had all kinds of imaginary characters that resided in me on a regular basis. As an only child for ten years, those "people" who only I could see became my entourage. They eagerly shared their hopes, dreams, triumphs, and disappointments, and I gladly wrote it all down. As time went on, I had quite the collection. More importantly, I knew I wanted to be an author, an entertainer through the written word.

After that revealing summer, later in the fall in seventh grade, my English teacher assigned a creative writing project. At the time, I was shy and introverted, but my writing allowed me to be free. What I could not say verbally, I could express through the power of the pen.

I was so excited to show her my book of poems. Yes, she would be blown away by my assignment, and more importantly, she would know my name, as I was the one who tried to become invisible in large settings, unsure of myself. I was uncomfortable in my skin, being awkwardly tall and lanky, blossoming prominently up top, and felt I stood out for all the wrong reasons.

I was too young to understand that I was one of God's divine masterpieces and did not have enough knowledge to walk in that power and truth. Yet, I handed in that assignment with high expectations. I was pleased with the final product, and I wanted that teacher also to be proud to have me as a student.

The day the assignment was returned, I waited with great anticipation, nerves tingling and on edge. The teacher walked around, placing assignments on desks, with routine casualness. When it became my turn, I received mine last. She threw it on my desk like a frisbee and announced to the class of over 30 kids that she was not grading it. I tried to protest, but she shut that down with her venomous tone, practically spitting at me, "You know it's plagiarized!"

My lips quivered as I struggled to utter, "No, it's not," but it came out about as loud as someone with laryngitis.

She turned on her heels as her face contorted into a grimace, shouting, "Shut up! You're getting a zero!"

I was embarrassed and humiliated; my body was shivering as if a sub-zero wind had engulfed my being. I sat there in disbelief as tears welled up in my eyes. I gathered my things and dragged myself to the next period, where I cowered at the lunch table in utter defeat and emotional pain.

My sandwich sat untouched, and when my classmates asked to see the poems, I was hesitant but still looking for validation. I passed it to them, and after a quick review, they responded, "Oh, you must have remembered these from somewhere."

Twice, in the span of an hour, I was crushed. The message was clear: I was not talented enough to write poetry or anything for that matter. I was untrustworthy. I was so inept; I had to steal them and pretend it was my work.

I arrived home shattered. I barely made it through the front door before breaking down. I collapsed into my mother's arms, crying hysterically.

It's a good thing we didn't need bail money for my mom, who promptly set up an appointment with the school's guidance counselor. We sat there with the counselor while I felt like the world was ending. You see, my mother was a Mama Bear—and coming for her children turned her into more of a *grizzly bear*. I feared what was to come and then what would be left behind.

The counselor had no explanation as we waited for the teacher to arrive. I sat in that chair vibrating like a silenced cell phone; my right leg bounced up and down like a jackhammer. Through the small glass window of the office door, I could see the teacher coming while my heart pounded in my chest.

My mother cut her eyes at me and commanded, "Calm yourself down." But I couldn't do as she asked because the *calm train* had left the station and was flying down the track with no brakes.

The teacher arrived and barely acknowledged our presence. The counselor gave a brief recap of events and then asked her directly, "Can you let us know why you assigned a failing grade?"

She uttered one sentence: "I don't have to put up with this," and she turned on her evil heels and left the office.

My grade was changed, but the damage was done. What some people don't understand is that words can cause physical pain and leave an imprint on your memory. The teacher's words were like daggers, which was confirmed by my peers. The way that we speak to our children, and each other, can have far-reaching implications for how we view ourselves, what we believe, how we treat others, and how we act.

From that point on, I didn't want to share my work with anyone for fear of being rejected again. That woman's words had me trapped in her mental prison. I walked around in her truth. I embraced her rejection and buried my God-given talent deep within my soul. She was supposed to be an authority figure, someone with influence, and she wielded her power over my fragile headspace.

Years passed—three decades, no exaggeration. I was successful in my day job, but that constant gnawing in my gut was with me from sunrise to sunset. That small whisper would not go away, constantly urging me to release my gifts and talents and to embrace my purpose.

The reason why I say "release" is because, after that terrible event, I never stopped writing. Even though I was determined not to be hurt again, writing oozed out of my pores. It's part of my DNA, the way I was knitted in the womb. I continued to write and squander my works inside a plastic bag, including short stories, novels, songs, plays, and poems. I carried that plastic bag from house to house and state to state. Now and then, I'd pull out the writings and muse over their worth and promptly return them to that safe place.

Sadly, we become comfortable in our chaos. We start to believe this is the way it is. So, *I'd better get used to it and just accept it.* Meanwhile, we're helping everyone else live out their hopes and dreams while ours lay in a manmade crypt. To actually change our circumstances takes courage and a conscious decision to no longer allow someone else to dictate who we are or what we're supposed to be doing. Getting out of that place of despair usually requires a jolt to our everyday routine, something that sounds the alarm and makes you pay attention.

For me, it was just that! I received an unexpected phone call from an old colleague I had not spoken to for a long time. We were having a great conversation, but then she made an announcement: She published a book.

Once I received those words, it sent a shock through my system. It was such a lightning bolt to my spirit, and I promptly hung up after a curt goodbye. I was angry with God—no, I was furious, and I wanted answers. I needed Him to explain to me how He allowed her to become an author when it was my lifelong dream. It was my destiny, not hers. I blamed God for delaying my dreams, and in the midst of wailing, my own burning bush spoke to me with conviction and said, *Did I say you could not write? Who said you were not worthy? Who have you been listening to?*

My God! The wake-up call does not adequately explain what happened that night in my pitch-black dining room, where I laid on the floor near a mental breakdown. My mind was blown by the clarity of His voice, and in that instant, the chains were broken, and my inner fears were released.

It begs the question: Who do we listen to, and who or what do we allow inside our head and in our space?

Listen, this is so very important. There are haters out there who have broken souls. They could be teachers, parents, guardians, bosses, or managers who've been through Hell and back. If they're not healed, you may get the brunt of their pain. Watching you excel while they are stuck in their own rut just fuels their anger, so they lash out and tear down your confidence.

Along with the haters, some people either don't see your light or can't understand your assignment. They can't handle seeing you get ahead or hearing you share your vision. In other words, who are you to think you can be a successful entrepreneur, artist, actor, fashion designer, engineer, and so on?

Over the years, I've spoken to many people whose lives were crushed by what someone said they couldn't do or couldn't be, and it changed them and altered their divine pathway. When they share their truth, there is a sadness in their eyes, and it pains me to see another flower was destroyed at the root.

Some of us can withstand the storm and come back stronger, but everybody is not built that way.

I'm sure you have encountered that unruly customer service agent or a rude waiter. These are service-oriented jobs I greatly respect and appreciate. But when there is a disconnect, you can see there is no joy in what they're doing; it's just superficial and methodical. They are earning a paycheck, finding ways to exist, *but they are not truly living.* Some people feel it's too late and walk around in defeat because no one was there to tell them any different.

Can you imagine knowing you're planted in the wrong garden and thinking there's nothing you can do about it? I'm here to tell you that it's only too late if you have created your own internal glass ceiling, which is what I did. For me, it wasn't that my family and friends didn't have my back, but they could not repair the hurt to my soul. I had work to do to get back on track, but the key here is my gift never left me.

Some of you know your gift is waiting on you to give it life but to compensate, you've been serving on every mission board, church committee, volunteering, helping others with their hopes, goals, and dreams while forsaking your own! Your heart's desire still remains and nudges at you ever so slightly as a reminder that what has been divinely given to you was not in vain.

There is no time machine to change the past, but you have the power to change the future. When I look back over the years of living in fear of rejection, I did myself a disservice while giving that teacher the victory. I essentially allowed her actions to shape my own when the truth of the matter probably was that she couldn't have written a poem to save her life, so why would she have given me any credit or encouragement? She could not see my light because of her own darkness. But when you are a child, already insecure and still finding your way, it's easy to get lost. But as I matured and grew in my faith, it was clear that what God places on your heart, no one can take away.

After walking in someone else's shoes for a long time, moving into your divine purpose takes courage but also a desire to live your authentic life. Initially, it won't be easy because you are still going to encounter haters, naysayers, and doubters, especially when they start to see you making that transition into your rightful place in the world. Some "friends" may even fall to the wayside, but you have to understand that everyone in your circle is not necessarily in your corner, and creating some distance and some space is required so you can really focus on your next level of living and owning your purpose. There are many ways to start activating your purpose. A great jumpstart is a vision board.

THE TOOL

A vision board can help you map out your right now and where you want to be. It's a constant reminder of your goals, along with achievable milestones.

The items you'll need are simple and can be found in most stores. Think of it as a fun arts and crafts project, but you don't need to be artistic to get this done. You can use a large poster board, notebook, or journal. Colored markers, highlighters, glue, old magazines, stickers, and other creative objects will help your dream visually come to life. Posting your board in a visible location (office, library, closet) will serve as a constant reminder to work towards your end goal(s).

This initial vision board will be for thirty days. You may think you have to put your whole life trajectory on the board – which is common, but for this moment in time, I'm going to advise you to start with small goals so you can get quick wins.

Think about where you are right now and what steps are needed to begin living and working on your purpose. Don't overthink it. For example, it could depict these steps/goals, but make it your own:

Step 1: Meditate/pray/discern over this new adventure in your life. Seek clarity and be at peace.

Step 2: Share with close friends and family what you believe your purpose is and that you're ready to move forward and would like their support.

Step 3: Investigate what would be needed to get this dream off the ground, i.e., budget, time, research, staffing, business plan, etc.

Step 4: Network with like-minded individuals and organizations for ideas and support.

Once you achieve each goal, mark it off and celebrate. Then move on to the next one. Believe me, thirty days is going to go by quickly and if you don't achieve all of the goals, carry it over for another thirty days, and please give yourself a lot of grace. When you fulfill all goals, create new ones.

After I had that life-changing moment, I was set free. It felt so good to be released from [wo]man's ideas and be in alignment with my divine pathway. No, it was not easy, but once those shackles were broken, I could move forward and not look back.

Today, I'm an award-winning author, writing coach, ghostwriter, and speaker. My journey was delayed but not denied. God truly will grant the desires of your heart if you let Him!

I want to encourage you to find a way to change your testimony if you wake up every day knowing you are not living out your purpose. Become intentional and be bold. Do it afraid. The road may be rocky; you may stumble and fall, but know you are an integral link in this great circle of life. You are needed, and I'm rooting for you. The world is waiting.

 **JC Gardner** is an international author, speaker, writing coach, and ghostwriter. Helping aspiring authors bring their projects to life through her coaching program is a blessing and a gift. She has written and co-authored numerous books and contributed to many publications. Her latest novel, "Heated," is an urban dramedy about a single mother's plight to do better despite her negative circumstances. It is the recipient of an IPPY Award, a Distinguished Author's Guild Award, and an Amazon bestseller.

JC was a closet writer for many years due to a devastating blow in her past that silenced her creativity and almost derailed her God-given talent of being an entertainer and storyteller through the written word. After a phenomenal, spiritual breakthrough, it was clear that what God has placed in your heart, no one can take away. After years of living in a cloud of self-doubt and fear of rejection, she uses her platform as a speaker to transform and empower women to reclaim their destiny using real-life examples, practical solutions, faith, and humor.

JC is a National Advisor at an international nonprofit. She has been married for over 35 years and has two successful grown children.

Stay in touch with JC:

https://www.facebook.com/AuthorJCG

https://www.instagram.com/author_jcg/

www.jc-gardner.com

authorjcg@yahoo.com

CHAPTER 9

BEATING THE ODDS

KEEPING YOUR FOCUS DURING EVERY CHALLENGE

Bessie Lee-Cappell, LSW, Inventor

MY STORY

Just like you, I've been through some very challenging moments in my life—challenging moments involving drugs, teen pregnancy, death, and other barriers that could have deterred me from success. Read on to find out what happened, and learn the tool I used to make it this far.

MY EARLIEST MEMORY (AGE FOUR)

I lived between two homes, my maternal grandparents and my maternal aunt Brenda's. A few years later, I found out that my grandparents and aunt petitioned family court for permanent legal custody.

I remember my siblings and I living at my aunt Brenda's house. Oh wait, did I mention I'm one of seven children. In fact, I'm the middle child! When I was four, my three oldest siblings lived with me at my aunt's house. One day, Children and Youth contacted my aunt Brenda regarding my mother's unknown whereabouts. They told my aunt Brenda that someone needed to provide care for my siblings, or they would end up in the foster care system. As a result, my aunt gained guardianship of my siblings.

We enjoyed block parties together and attending church. Even though those memories are vague, one memory in particular sticks out to me. My siblings and I are sitting in the hallway of my aunt's home. My siblings are sad, and all I can do is sit next to them, not quite understanding what's going on. My aunt asks them, "What's wrong?" My oldest sister says, "We want to live with my mom." My aunt says, "Are you sure? I don't want to hold you back from your mom, but you all can't keep coming back and forth, you understand?" My three siblings reply, "Yes." Since that day, we have never lived together with my aunt Brenda again.

THE BEGINNING OF RESPONSIBILITIES (AGE NINE)

Throughout the years, my siblings and mother would visit me in Philadelphia. In school, kids would ask me, "Where's your mom?" I didn't know what to say, so I wouldn't say anything. I lived between homes, as mentioned previously. When I lived with my grandparents, I had to help as much as possible because my grandmother was diabetic and immobile. She was diagnosed with polio as a little girl. I recall learning how to administer insulin to my grandmother, bathe her, comb her hair and occasionally go to the neighborhood corner store for her. My grandfather was the greatest man I ever knew! He cooked, cleaned, and catered to my grandmother daily! He was the perfect husband, grandfather, and father figure in my eyes.

WHERE WAS MY FATHER?

My mother met my father when she was 14, and he was 19 years old. When my mom was 19, she married my father and was soon pregnant with my oldest sister! My father struggled with addiction for most of my young childhood years. Once I hit my teenage years, he was in recovery. He took me out to the movies and dinner during his early recovery years. I was very uncomfortable with him because I didn't know him. I guess he felt like a stranger to me. I remember one outing, I was around the age of 12, and we were traveling on the train. A lady said to him, "Oh my God, she has to be your daughter because she looks just like you!" He says, "Really! You think we look alike?" I laughed it off because I thought he was joking. I soon realized it was not a joke. Days later, I hear my aunt Brenda on the telephone yelling. Later that day, my aunt came to me and explained that my dad wanted me to take a paternity test. My response was, "No." Throughout the years, I would not see my dad for months or even years at a time. If you think my childhood was a bit tough, let's fast forward to young adulthood.

COLLEGE SOPHOMORE YEAR

Towards the end of my sophomore year, amid a chaotic relationship, I found out that I was pregnant. I was 19 years old, scared, nervous, and I felt lost. I called my boyfriend, and he rushed home and found me crying. He consoled me and said, "It's going to be okay." I took six pregnancy tests which all came back positive. I also went to the nearby health clinic for confirmation. They counseled us on different options, including abortion. My boyfriend and I discussed the pregnancy and ultimately decided that we were going to embrace it.

After leaving the free health clinic, my boyfriend and I decided to tell our parents about the pregnancy. First stop was Aunt Brenda's house. I was nervous, but I told her about the pregnancy. Her reaction was calm, but she told me, "You will finish college." My boyfriend had to tell his mother the news. Her reaction was calm as well. Our parents were supportive; we moved from our apartment and in with my future mother-in-law.

TRAGEDY STRIKES

During the summer months of my pregnancy, I spent many days with my oldest sisters. I was emotional during my pregnancy, so relying on my older sisters for emotional support meant everything to me. One day, I went to my oldest sister's home to cry about my relationship with my boyfriend. She cried with me and told me it was going to be okay. She began singing gospel music. We ended that day laughing. About a week or so later, I woke up to a phone call from one of my cousins. She says, "Bessie, are you awake? I need you awake!" I said, "Yeah, what's up?" She says, "Your oldest sister died last night. Some people found her body washed up on the beach in Atlantic City."

All I could do was say, "No!" and scream. My boyfriend ran upstairs and asked me what happened as I cried hysterically. August 13, 2008, will always be ingrained in my head. That entire day, her story was all over every news channel. I was five months pregnant. Until this day, no one knows what happened to her. Life hasn't been the same for me since that day. Trying to stay focused on not miscarrying from the traumatic news, I thought about my unborn child. Keeping that at the forefront of my focus allowed me to keep my composure as best as I could.

COLLEGE JUNIOR YEAR

I entered my junior year of college with a big belly! Everyone stared at me. We found out we were having a girl! She was due December 31, 2008, which would allow me to complete my entire semester, go on winter break, and return for the spring semester. With this plan, I anticipated graduating on time. My daughter was born at 6:05 pm on December 18, 2008, six pounds, four ounces, 19 inches long. Remembering the specifics of the birth of my child meant and still means a lot to me. She was beautiful, and I could tell we would be best buddies for the rest of our lives. I contacted my student advisor regarding taking off the spring semester and returning for the summer sessions to graduate on time. After meeting with my advisor, I was told that I could take my spring classes in the summer and start my senior year classes on time to graduate. However, I was misinformed. When the summer classes began, I could not take the spring classes because they were not offered in the summer. As a result, I had to either change my major to sociology to graduate on time or graduate a year late. Being focused and passionate about starting what I finished and being focused on and passionate about social work, I decided to not switch my major and to graduate a year late. I graduated with my BSW in May of 2011. Now, let's fast forward a few years.

2016 A YEAR TO REMEMBER

February 14, 2016, is a day I will *never* forget! We all know February 14 for Valentine's Day, the day of love. I was excited for this day! I had a hair appointment and would get a nice, long, and luscious weave sew-in. I had two kids (one girl, age seven, and one boy, age three) at the time. My kids were in school; I was off from work and ready to celebrate Valentine's Day. I began to get my hair done, but I received a panic call from my older sister halfway through my sew-in. I answered the phone as usual, "Hey sistaaa," as she replied, "Bessie, this is serious. Tae is in the hospital! You need to head over there quickly! I was told that she wasn't breathing!" I screamed, *"What?!* I'm on my way now!" My little sister battled with kidney failure, and on that day, she was due to attend dialysis. However, hours before her appointment, too much fluid built up in her lungs, which caused shortness of breath.

The ambulance arrived at her home and found her unresponsive. By the time they reached the hospital, my sister was brain dead. The doctors did all they could, but it wasn't enough; she died minutes later. Talk about one of the worst days of my life thus far! We were the closest! I took another huge loss in my life that day. I had to break the news to my children. My daughter was heartbroken. She and I cried together as we held on to each other. My daughter was only seven years old. I couldn't imagine what my life would look like without another one of my siblings here. I never imagined our lives to look like this. I always imagined us getting older together, experiencing life together—all our children playing together, all of us vacationing together and attending family dinners. Now family gatherings would be very different. Valentine's day will *never* be the same for me.

Three months later, I completed graduate school. I was proud of my accomplishment but sad I didn't have my younger and oldest sister there to celebrate with me. Months after I graduated, I took the Licensure Social Work Exam, and I passed! Less than a year later, I was expecting my third child.

THE SCARE

August 2018, my youngest was born. I was prepared to breastfeed him as I did for my other children. However, latching was difficult for him. I never had an issue with my older two latching, I thought I was a pro! Because latching was difficult, I allowed the nursery to feed him formula the first night. It was a good thing I did. The nurses realized my baby's breathing was off. When I woke up in the morning and asked for my baby, the nurse brought him to me and said, "We're sending him to the NICU for monitoring. His breathing is off a bit, so we'll have him monitored."

She allowed me to kiss him and provided me with the NICU location and number. At first, I didn't think it was serious. This was all new to me.

My older children never went into the NICU. They were in the room with me, breastfed well, and went home with me at discharge. I wasn't prepared for this. My boyfriend and I went to visit our baby in the NICU. We didn't know he would be under a light, hooked to many tubes, have cloth-like sunglasses on, and loud surrounding monitors. We scrubbed our hands before entering and placed our phones in plastic bags. I was so scared for my baby.

A nurse came over and spoke to us. She explained the tubes, sunglasses, light, and monitor. The nurses were amazing and very helpful. I couldn't breastfeed him because of his breathing, but I could pump, and they fed him my breast milk through his feeding tube. I was sad. I went back to my room and cried. My boyfriend was sad too. I prayed and asked a few individuals to pray too. I didn't want to tell many people because I didn't want my anxiety to get out of hand. The uncertainty of the NICU is the most nerve-wracking situation I've ever been in.

Three days later, I was discharged from the hospital without my baby boy. I cried terribly when no one was around. All I could do was look at the bassinet in my bedroom and all the baby furniture in my home and think, *this isn't right coming home without my baby!* I cried out, "Why me, Lord? Haven't I been through enough? Please don't take my baby away from me, Lord!" Three days later, during our NICU visit with our baby, the doctor said, "He's going home with you guys today!" It was a total shock and the best news ever! Our baby came home. He had a visiting nurse the first week home and many follow-up doctor's appointments soon after. Overall, he was a healthy baby when he arrived home. The lesson of gratefulness and appreciation was surely learned. I always took for granted giving birth and walking out of the hospital with my children. I have heard of babies going to the NICU typically when there are early-onset pregnancy complications. I was most definitely in for an awakening. I requested Family Medical Leave from work for three months. Life became more chaotic with three children, a mortgage, daycare expenses, and much more upon my return to work. As a result, a new venture was born.

HOW THE BUSINESS/ENTREPRENEURIAL JOURNEY BEGAN

Two words: *Brush Bib*—my first invented product. I never envisioned myself as an inventor, but I always knew I was solution-focused. The Brush

Bib is a circular silicone barrier that goes around bottle brushes to prevent the user from being splashed on. While washing many bottles at home and work, I was tired of the water splatter stains on my clothing. As a result, I created a product to solve the issue. Initially, the Brush Bib was not intended as a business venture. However, a friend suggested I turn my invention into a business venture, so I did. Not knowing anything about being a business owner, I educated myself day by day. Throughout this journey, more tragedy struck (which you can learn more about later), but I remained focused. Two years later in business, I possess three Provisional Patent Applications, three invented products on the market, five trademarks, two baby product companies, and one nonprofit organization while working full-time as a social worker. All this has been achieved by remaining focused even through my challenges. It's not easy to keep your focus, especially when the odds seem to be against you and challenges arise. Allow me to provide the skills I use to remain focused.

THE TOOL

STEP 1:

One word: "Positivity." One may ask, "How can you remain positive with all the chaos? How do you remain positive when the odds are against you? How do you remain positive when dealing with challenging situations? How do you remain positive during a rocky relationship? How do you remain positive after the death of a loved one?" One thing for sure, it's not easy!

In my chapter, you've learned about the many challenges I've been subjected to. You also learned that I kept moving forward. In each situation, I always look for the good. Looking for the good in a bad situation is far from easy, but it must be done to progress.

When I lost my oldest sibling, I focused on my unborn child's beauty and upcoming birth. When I found out that I wasn't going to graduate college on time, I thought to myself, you made it this far, don't turn around now.

When I lost my younger sibling, I thought to myself, *stay strong for your children and your family.* I also thought to myself, *your sister was tired of fighting her illness, and now she's in a better place.*

I'm a true believer that without positivity, you cannot move forward for productivity! No productivity equals no success! Positivity is a practice of optimism in your attitude. Practice positivity in your daily life.

Start with this daily technique: Close your eyes, take a deep breath and exhale. Again, breathe in and release. Breathe in and exhale again. While keeping your eyes closed, remember your one desired goal. Remember why you set this specific goal. Keep those eyes closed. Now, envision the happiness you feel now that the goal is accomplished. Envision the happiness of those you love around you. With your eyes remaining closed, start smiling while you envision your achievement. Remember, it's okay to cry as well. Take another deep breath in and exhale. Open your eyes. Now say to yourself, "I am strong, I can, and I will do this." Tell yourself that you are achieving this goal for yourself and call out those names of individuals who you want to benefit from your success. This technique may need to be practiced a couple of times each day in the midst of a challenge.

If you can master this first step, you will be ready to move forward with the next step!

For more information, you can email info@babybottlebrushbib.com

Facebook: Bessie Lee-Cappell

I believe I was conceived in October of 1987. I was told that my mother contemplated the pregnancy; however, on June 21, 1988, in Hahnemann hospital, Bessie Lee was born (prematurely is what I was told by my maternal aunt Brenda). My mom used to think that I was born on June 22, 1988 at Penn Hospital, but my grandparents begged to differ.

I was born ____ pounds and ___ ounces. I was ___ inches long. You can fill in the blanks because hell if I know. Most mothers remember the weight and height of their babies, but I didn't have the luxury of having this information. Approximately two days after my birth, my mother was discharged from the hospital; however, she was an active drug user, so the hospital refused to release me to her. She left me in the hospital, and the staff contacted my maternal grandparents Nathaniel and Bessie Lee King.

Nathaniel was cooking dinner when he received the call. He rushed to the hospital with my aunt Vera. The doctor told my grandfather, "She's a crack baby. Are you sure you want a crack baby?" His response was, "She's my granddaughter!" My new home was 5641 N Warnock Street, Philadelphia, PA, 19120.

Being born prematurely and as a crack baby had some setbacks. According to my grandmother, I cried a lot and had a bad hip. She said she rubbed and molded my hip with her bare hands every day until it went into place. Some doctors thought I wouldn't walk, but because of my grandmother, she proved them different! My entire life has been "different." I've been beating the odds since birth. I am now 33 years old—a mother, wife, business owner of two companies, and a social worker.

CHAPTER 10

PERSEVERANCE

HOW TO BUILD AND EMPOWER YOUR COMMUNITY

Melissa A. Washington

MY STORY

If you asked me in 2015 where I would be in the next few years, it would not be where I am today. As I look back on my life leading up to 2015, I can pinpoint all of the steppingstones which allowed me to follow my calling and find success doing it. Today, I can proudly say, I am building a community around the country to empower women veterans. A significant part of my role is sharing what I've learned with others. Knowledge is power, and by empowering my fellow women veterans, we can collectively make changes and help others thrive.

When aiming to make any change within a community, it is vital to take a hands-on approach. I always make sure to have my boots on the ground and a seat at the table. I do not wait to be invited and, on many occasions, have invited myself. One of my favorite quotes is from Shirley Chisholm, the first black woman in Congress: "If they don't give you a seat at the table, bring a folding chair." For me, there is nothing worse than walking into a room full of old white guys. Yes, this has happened to me many times. It is imperative to diversify the conversation—inviting women, people of color, members of the LGBTQ+ community, and the disabled to offer their voices. All of us need to be in the room with the decision-makers.

As you might have guessed, I am not one to stand on the sidelines. But it's so easy for people to complain about something, rather than be part of making it better. Change requires time, energy, and emotional labor. And so, the first question you must ask yourself is: what do I want to create? Next, you must determine your level of involvement. Don't be afraid to ask for help. Invite others who want to be a part of the change. Find people whose skill sets complement yours, so you can collaborate and make your presence in your community a solid one.

So many women want to be part of the change, in one form or another, but do not know how or where to start. I hope my story, and the tools I discuss below, will help inspire you to build and empower your own community.

In 2014, the one thing I could not find in the greater Sacramento region was a group specifically for women veterans, as joining the "good ol' boys club" was not what I was looking for. As a Navy veteran, I wanted to connect with other women who had served. I called the local veteran's hospital, where they referred me to their women's health clinic. The only group was an MST (Military Sexual Trauma) support group which was not what I was looking for. I searched the internet to see what other groups were out there locally and found nothing.

Build it, and they will come.

And so, if you cannot find it, build it yourself, which is exactly what I did. In December, I sent out emails to women veterans and supporters I knew and posted on social media, asking friends and family to spread the word about a new women veterans networking group.

For our first get-together, in January 2015, we met at a Mexican restaurant in Sacramento. I chose this location as it was centrally located and had easy access off the freeway. It also offered a separate meeting space with a long table, free parking, and they were able to accommodate separate checks. I wanted to remove any potential barriers which might keep women from attending.

The synergy was amazing, with most of them not even knowing each other before that night. We could have easily closed the restaurant down.

All branches, officers, and enlisted were in attendance. After the first dinner, we decided to meet on the third Thursday of every month and continue to meet on this day. The meetups would be open only to women who had served or are currently serving.

We discussed where to meet the following month and shared ideas for potential speakers. We rotated to different local restaurants during the first few meetups until we found a corporate meeting space. Initially, my intent for these meetings was more of a hobby, where I would facilitate a local community networking group that would meet once a month. Yet, I soon realized there was a broader need for women veterans to connect. Not long after, we scaled nationally.

The group was originally called "Women Veterans Professional Networking," but there was a conflict with another group in the San Francisco Bay area. After a bit of research, I changed the name to Women Veterans Alliance (WVA). We wanted our model to be different from the traditional veteran organizations, which provided obstacles. While many veteran groups are set up to help individuals experiencing disabilities, homelessness, or military sexual trauma, they often have a variety of formalities they must follow.

Initially, I went in thinking I could do it all. But I soon realized I needed to do what was in my wheelhouse. With my background in human resources and corporate recruiting and owning a small business, I could offer my entrepreneurship, networking, and professional development expertise.

I did have a slight advantage when it came to getting WVA off the ground. Several years earlier, I began connecting with people and organizations in the veteran space while serving on the California Interagency Council on Veteran Affairs. I also taught LinkedIn classes at the Employment Development Department (EDD)'s VetNet program and helped transition service members and their spouses at Beale Air Force Base, which I still do.

But it was still a challenge to find more women veterans beyond my initial contacts. So once again, I used another skillset of mine: LinkedIn. In addition to working for the company for several years and planning their global corporate events, I've long offered seminars on how to maximize LinkedIn for job searches and recruitment. My 2014 book, *Get Back to Work: Smart & Savvy Real-World Strategies to Make Your Next Career Move*, also includes a variety of tips and tricks for the platform.

I searched for local women veterans using several search terms—specifically their location and past employer (military branch). It was interesting to find a lot of women who served did not identify themselves as a veteran on their LinkedIn profiles. When it became too time-consuming to scroll past profile after profile of male veterans, I also began including the words 'she' or 'her' in my searches. Eventually, my hard work paid off. I started to find these gems on the platform, and, to this day, I still have a lot of success using LinkedIn to connect with new women veterans.

Like many entrepreneurs, I initially used the self-funded model for WVA. I invested my time and money to create a website, branding, social media presence, and everything else which goes into starting a business. WVA was my purpose: an opportunity to channel my passion for helping others. But enthusiasm won't sustain a business—you must have a revenue stream. As the community grew, I began implementing a membership program, eventually pushing me from excel spreadsheets to a membership software program.

As our meetups grew, I received interest from the civilian community. This led to our Mix & Mingle (M&M) events, which serve as a wonderful way for women veterans to connect with the local community and vice versa. Unlike our monthly meetups, these quarterly events are open to the public and include refreshments and raffle prizes. From the very beginning, our M&M events were incredibly popular—so much so, they inspired us to add to our signature annual event: the Unconference.

The Unconference was not only born from a desire to take WVA to the next level but also as a way to channel another passion of mine: producing events. My experience at LinkedIn had given me the tools to create a larger opportunity for the organization, one which would bring women veterans together from across the United States while also generating revenue to support our day-to-day efforts in local communities.

People often ask about the name Unconference. My answer, simply put, is, "It's not your typical conference." Having attended, planned, and spoken at countless conferences over the years, I purposefully designed the Unconference to include the best elements of these events. I wanted to offer our women veterans an elevated, three-day experience. Our inaugural Northern California Women Veterans Unconference took place in 2016, and it was a huge success, with over 200 women veterans in attendance.

But it was also a learning experience, with a lot of sacrifice on my part. For instance, I had set the cost of admission far too low, as I assumed I would be able to find sponsors to offset fees. Unfortunately, I did not have luck securing enough sponsors and paid the difference out of my pocket.

Still, I went ahead with planning 2017's Unconference, this time removing the wording "Northern California" from the title, as we were attracting women from all over the state. We also held two regional events: a springtime Unconference in Sacramento and one in Southern California in the fall. The following year, I learned one annual Unconference was best, as was geographical diversification. And so, we moved forward, taking what we learned and incorporating new ideas into each following year. In 2018, the Unconference took place in Southern California, while in 2019, it was in Monterey. 2021, meanwhile, expanded to Las Vegas. Each year, the Unconference has grown to include new activities, including art classes, wine tasting, golf lessons, childcare, movie premieres, comedy nights, massages, clothing boutiques, and more.

2018's Unconference, in particular, marked a special milestone for WVA, establishing the Melissa Washington Small Business Award to address the inequities in funding for women veteran entrepreneurs. The same year, I founded Women Veterans Giving, a non-profit that creates programs to empower and fund women veterans' business endeavors while helping them gain valuable experience serving as board members.

When we established a committee to review applications for the inaugural award, they came up with the title. My fellow veterans told me, "If it was not for you, we wouldn't be here." It was a powerful and rewarding moment for me. Now, several years later, we have given more than $15,000 to help women veterans expand their businesses. The program has evolved year-over-year with workshops, coaching, and funding opportunities.

While I could not be prouder of how far WVA and WVG have come, the road was not easy. There were *many* days at the beginning where I wanted to quit. Once, a member went to a meeting at one of the traditional veteran organizations and shared information about WVA. A man there had the audacity to tell her, "You ladies won't last." Moments like that fuel my fire. But there are certainly days when someone may not be nice, or when I am told "No," or I make a misstep. These are all experiences from which to learn and grow. One of my missteps, for instance, happened early on.

I often hear from businesses interested in connecting with woman veterans, so I created WX (Women's Exchange) with the name to relate to the military store's PX, BX, and NEX. As you might imagine, the short-lived URL I chose, womveteransexchange.com, did not go over very well. It was not until I got an email from someone about the word "sex" in the URL, I realized my oversight. It was an innovative idea with the wrong wording. In its place, I established the Women Veteran Online Business Directory, which lives on the WVA website for women veteran business owners to advertise their products and services. However, despite the initial "oops" moment, the directory quickly grew as an outlet to empower women veterans while producing an additional sales funnel for women who have their business listed.

In the building of this community, I also added an online store with women veteran-specific merchandise for all of us to wear proudly. Most women veterans do not wear hats or shirts which recognize they have served. If an item is worn, they will likely be asked about their husband's service. It can be difficult to find items specifically for women veterans, and I wanted to make it easier to increase our visibility. Additionally, I offer women veteran authors the chance to sell their books through our site, while I added an Allies Directory for organizations that focus predominantly on women veterans.

THE TOOL

BE PART OF THE COMMUNITY

Building visibility and a community starts with action. It's crucial to incorporate the public to build awareness. Several years ago, women veterans took to the field of a Sacramento River Cats game to lead Take Me Out to the Ballgame during the seventh-inning stretch. It was a memorable moment that also created awareness of our organization.

In 2016, we collected back scratchers, bags, lap blankets, lotions, reading glasses, scarves, slippers, and socks. After assembling items at our first Unconference in Sacramento, we donated them to women veterans at assisted living facilities throughout the region. These ladies were not only a hoot, but they were also so thankful to receive something they could use (not a man's razor or size eleven socks). In 2018, we were the partner organization for the city of Sacramento's Veterans Day Parade, whose theme was Celebrating Military Women: Past, Present, and Future. I was honored to be included on the planning committee.

Building a wider community is also about connecting with others when I travel. I have hosted women veteran "popup" meetups in Los Angeles, Dallas, Miami, and Las Vegas, among other areas. If you're interested in facilitating a popup meetup:

- Look for a restaurant or meeting space that can accommodate the group.
- Schedule for a specific date.
- Send a targeted email blast to the area and post it on social media.
- Bring along some small give-away items.

Keep moving and growing.

Over these last few years, I have become an influencer in the veteran community, as well as the go-to person when it comes to women veterans. Being seen as a leader in the community brings opportunities to speak at events and appear on TV, radio, and podcast interviews. But I didn't just want to wait for other media outlets to knock. On my "to do" list for the first couple of years was to publish a magazine. I eventually crossed it off as I was not able to make the time, nor did I have the experience. Looking back, I realized the timing wasn't right. Now, nearly seven years after launching WVA, the moment has come. We've partnered with a woman veteran-owned publisher, and I'm proud to say, *Women Veterans Magazine California Edition* will launch in the early part of 2022, with versions for additional states to follow.

Listening to and understanding the needs of women veterans helped me build this community. Together, we created a safe and fun environment that encourages camaraderie amongst sisters, allowing us to share resources, make new friends, and support one another. Along the way, WVA has empowered its members to start their own businesses while supporting products and services offered by other women veterans.

Today, Women Veterans Alliance is the premier national network focused on directly impacting the quality of life of women veterans. We do this successfully by connecting the community directly and bringing people and programs together through a reliable and resourceful platform.

A few parting thoughts:

Pray about everything in whatever shape or form that means to you. I need to remember to breathe properly. Sometimes, I am moving so fast in my life; I am actually taking short breaths (which is not healthy). Finally, an Army veteran and good friend of mine, Lila Holley, shared these wise words with me, which I keep on my desk: "Focus your energy on your mission and let your actions and character speak volumes to those who are assigned on your journey."

Interested in learning more about how to become a leader in your community? Check out my eBook to learn more: WomenVeteransAlliance.com/ebook.

Visit these websites for more information on women veterans:

WomenVeteransAlliance.com

WomenVeteransGiving.org

WomenVeteransMagazine.com

Award-winning advocate, speaker, author, entrepreneur, CEO, and proud Navy veteran **Melissa A. Washington** wears many hats, yet woven throughout her diverse pursuits are a mission of service and a passion for empowering her fellow women.

As an in-demand speaker whose topics range from career reinvention and women veterans to discovering one's self-worth, Melissa has shared valuable insight from her multi-faceted career—presenting for the likes of Marriott, the Urban League, and IMEX America. Melissa has also appeared on the *Dr. Phil Show*, *The Balancing Act*, and on SiriusXM, ABC, NBC, CBS, and Fox.

Following a decade in corporate recruiting and human resources, Melissa founded her own consulting service, which helps businesses and individuals hire talent, search for jobs, and more. She is also the author of *Get Back to Work: Smart & Savvy Real-World Strategies to Make Your Next Career Move*.

Additionally, Melissa is the founder and CEO of Women Veterans Alliance—a national organization that seeks to empower and positively impact the lives of women veterans and its non-profit wing, Women Veterans Giving. In 2021, Melissa expanded her role in the community by co-founding *Women Veterans Magazine*, the first publication of its kind to serve California's more than 165,000 women veterans.

A longtime resident of Northern California, Melissa was a 2011 recipient of the *Sacramento Business Journal's* prestigious 40 Under 40 award and was among the *Journal's* Women Who Mean Business honorees in 2017. She has also been recognized by the National Association of Women Business Owners with an Outstanding Women Leader Visionary Award and received the 2016 Soroptimist Ruby Award, which recognizes women helping women. In 2019, she received the Center for Women Veterans' Trailblazer Award, and in 2021, she received the National Women of Influence Veteran of Influence Award.

CHAPTER 11

YOU'RE GONNA MAKE IT

HOW TO BOLDLY EMBRACE LIFE'S TRANSITIONS

Rosalind Beresford, ICC-IPC

MY STORY

It was spring 1972. I was ten years old. I was awakened from sleep and given a small, soft-sided, orange, and olive-green flowered suitcase packed with my clothes. It was quite fashionable in that late 60s early 70s flower power kind of way. Under ordinary circumstances, I would have been quite pleased to receive it. But this whole event was far from ordinary; it was a little scary.

My mother whisked all seven of her children out the door in the dark of night and into a waiting car. There was an eerie, tense silence in the car as our pastor drove us to the military base in Halifax, Nova Scotia. I suspect my older siblings knew what was happening, but I was in the dark, and so were my younger siblings. Our destination was unknown. No one spoke.

For the first time in my life, I boarded an airplane. It was a loud and sparsely furnished military plane. I could hear my rapidly beating heart above the roar of the engines. I had no idea where we were going or what lay ahead.

We flew for several hours through the dark of night. The sun was coming up when we deplaned. I didn't know it at the time, but we had arrived in Trenton, Ontario—another military base.

We were shown to the terminal. I spotted a very close family friend. I practically ran through a window to get to him for a hug. His family had always been part of our lives on the military base in Bagotville, Quebec. The familiarity was comforting after hours of tense silence.

We stayed with these close family friends overnight. The next morning, lugging the flowered suitcase, we boarded a bus. The trip was slightly more comfortable than a military plane, but fear enveloped me. Our destination was Kitchener, Ontario.

We were met by a man I did not know: my mother's brother. The eight of us lived for several weeks with my uncle and his family as my mother searched for a job and a home for us.

The contents of that flowered suitcase were the only remnants of a former chapter of my life as a military brat and daughter of a raging, abusive, alcoholic father. I didn't know it then, but my mother had the courage to embrace change to save her life and the lives of her seven children aged four and a half years to 15 years.

This new chapter held a lot of unknowns, but fear was loosening its grip. It was the first time in my life that fear did not rule the household.

We settled in a walk-up three-bedroom apartment. My possessions started to grow from the contents of that flowered suitcase to include a foam mattress on the floor in my bedroom, which I shared with my younger sister, schoolbooks, and library books. Over the year or so in that small apartment, my mother managed to scrounge together some new personal possessions to add some comfort to this new chapter of my life.

To this day, I can picture that olive green and orange colored, soft-sided flowered suitcase. I think of it as a symbol of freedom. A symbol of stepping into the unknown to find a happier chapter of my life, thanks to my mother's courage to embrace change and become the hero of her own life and my hero.

I admired my mother's strength, but I also believed that because she allowed herself to be tied to marriage and domesticity, she became a victim. I watched *The Mary Tyler Moore Show* avidly. It was a show about a

20-something woman pursuing a career, living a glamorous life, free of the socially accepted constraints of marriage and motherhood. I bought into the feminist agenda that we don't need a man to be happy. Yet, my high school boyfriend's *Leave It to Beaver* family offered me something I had never known before—stability and security.

That high school boyfriend stuck around and was patient as I dreamed of being Mary Tyler Moore. Eventually, I at least partially bought into his family's ideals, and I married him at age 24. Looking back, that is where I started losing my self-imagined identity as a strong, independent woman who was going to turn the world on with her smile and take the town—if not the world—by storm.

Change is a paradox. You can both want and fear it at the same time.

I was someone who was used to change. Change revolved around me my whole life. As a military brat, I moved five times before I was ten. Between the age of 10 and 17, I moved five more times. As a university student, I moved every four months. As a wife and mother of two, I moved nine times, seven of those moves were international.

One thing all those moves had in common was my ability to start over. These changes provided me with so many great opportunities. I had a great excuse to redecorate my home every few years. I was able to meet new people from all over the world, explore new cultures and exotic locations, and start over with a clean slate.

Even with all that change, I was able to find stability. I was able to reinvent myself many times to suit the new neighborhood, culture, and host country. I was able to morph all that experience with change into a career as an intercultural trainer for multi-national corporations and expat coach to people moving to new countries. Change, while scary, has many rewards.

I knew how to manage change, and yet, when I badly wanted to get out of a marriage haunted by my husband's multiple infidelities, the very idea of making that change felt overwhelming. Leaving my marriage scared me even though I knew making that change was my best option to find happiness. I knew from my mother's example that it was possible to become the hero of my own life, but I felt paralyzed and uncertain. I felt like I didn't have many choices. I wondered, *why do I fear to change?* I sought answers with the help of a therapist. Here is what I learned about change and why it is so difficult to navigate.

Change is risky. When your brain senses risk, your defense mechanism kicks in. Your brain becomes flooded with dopamine, and it looks for corrective actions it can trigger. Your brain encourages every available neuron to regain control and is wired to provide answers to uncertainty. It wants you to do anything to reduce the stress—your brain defaults to the easiest and least painful option. The easiest solution is to stay in your comfort zone. I stayed in my comfortable, unhappy marriage.

Uncertainty is more stressful than predictable negative outcomes. Think about that. We'd rather face predictable negative outcomes than face uncertainty and risk that something good could happen. I finally understood what drove me to search for the evidence of his multiple infidelities. No matter how devastated, disrespected, and unhappy I would feel, at least I would know for sure. That pain I felt in the moment of discovery somehow satisfied my need to be certain. For 20 years, it wasn't enough to get me to make a change though, because my life, while painful, was also comfortable because it was familiar.

The unknown is scary. Change is all about moving into the unknown. Fear causes unclear and irrational thinking and behavior. You end up staying in unhappy and unhealthy situations.

Your brain hates loss, especially when you have an emotional investment. You don't want to lose all the time and effort you've already exerted. Your brain's desire for loss aversion means you will likely make choices to avoid change. Aversion to loss can cause logic to fly out the window. My brain was convinced I would lose everything I had enjoyed for the past 30 years.

Your brain expects things to stay the same. Change challenges the information stored in your brain, and trust is broken. Any change inconsistent with your core beliefs will be scary and stressful. You develop core beliefs about how the world is supposed to work just by living that way for an extended period. Change challenges that. By my late 40s my identity had morphed into expat wife and mother. It was a comfortable and rewarding life. My brain wanted my life to stay that way.

You're so afraid of what others will think you're afraid to try. My brain convinced me that family and friends would judge me as foolish for the choices I made to stay despite the infidelities.

Your brain may tell you stories. My biggest fear was that I wouldn't survive and thrive. My brain convinced me I would return to my childhood's unstable and subsistence lifestyle if I chose to change my marital status. You become convinced that the lies your brain is telling you are truths. Your brain weaves a story about horrible consequences as means to get you to jump back to your comfort zone because it is safer there than it is on the other side of change.

We equate change with mistakes. In my mind, if I left my husband, that would mean that over half of my life had been a mistake.

Maybe you can relate to not feeling good enough, not smart enough. Maybe you feel like the devil you know is better than the devil you don't. You wonder, *what if I fail?* I know change can be scary, but I also know that everything you want is on the other side of that fear. I challenge you to imagine instead that you fly. I will share my secret to managing change with you.

Because my brain was doing its job, I found myself afraid to embrace the very thing that I knew had saved my mother's life all those years ago. I was resisting change, but I was the kid who wanted to be the carefree, adventurous Mary Tyler Moore.

I found myself grappling with chronic infidelity and suffering in silence, making myself sick so I could continue living a very comfortable, unhappy life.

Once I learned that my brain was trying to protect me, I began to understand how I could find myself struggling to master my fear of change, despite a history of embracing change.

My crisis point came during Christmas 2014. I had spent the last year shuffling back and forth between trying to start a new life with my unfaithful husband in another new country and my childhood home, which despite the death of my beloved stepfather and the grave illness of my very needy mother, was my safe haven. It was my escape from unhappiness. It was my dream board, and I could imagine a life in my hometown.

That Christmas, my millionaire's family, two kids, and an incredibly successful husband spent two weeks together being the picture-perfect family. Inside I was dying. I pretended to myself, my kids, my friends, and my extended family that all was good. It wore me out. I became physically, mentally, and emotionally exhausted. My health went downhill. Fear showed its ugly face in every area of my life. It was stressful and debilitating, and I was at the end of my rope.

Many of us choose fear. We allow fear to disguise itself as practicality. Was I going to choose fear, or was I going to choose to become the hero of my own life and embrace change?

I realized that the very thing that was going to save me was also the thing that I feared the most. After all, hadn't my mother saved her life and mine because she had the courage to embrace change? Could I leave a life of stability and security for a new, unknown life that I understood would make me a happier, healthier person? I decided that even if I ended up having to be a barista in a coffee shop to make ends meet, I was going to be happier. I was going to embrace my inner Mary Tyler Moore. I began to hum the theme for the Mary Tyler Moore show regularly.

So, where was that young girl who wanted to be Mary Tyler Moore? I traded my soul for security and stability, but my soul wanted to fly, and it did. I knew I was not going to resist change again.

THE TOOL

Where did that courage come from? Looking back, I realize specific actions I took allowed me to manage my fear and live in the unknown.

I embraced change, and you can too using the following six steps.

C - Control negative thoughts.

H - Have confidence in yourself.

A - Allow yourself to freak out. Feel the fear!

N - Narrate your own story.

G - Go nuts. Invite excitement in.

E - Evaluate what you are feeling.

For the purpose of this chapter, I'm going to concentrate on helping you learn to control your negative thoughts.

The first step to taking control of your negative thoughts is to become familiar with your negative chatterbox. The voice in your head that speaks to you in a manner that you would never speak to someone else. Name it; make friends with it. This exercise helps you become aware of when your negative chatterbox is influencing your thinking. If you know it well, it is easier to identify when it has taken over your thoughts. Have a conversation with it. What proof is there that the thoughts are true? Are the thoughts real or imagined?

Once you've become familiar with your chatterbox, the next step is to use The Stop Method to take control of it. Develop a stop mechanism. This can take any form that works for you. It can be verbal: you just say "Stop!" out loud. It can be more physical: Get up and walk around, take some deep cleansing breaths. A more extreme kinetic method is to wear an elastic band around your wrist and snap it when you start hearing your negative chatterbox.

Part of controlling your negative chatterbox is to feel safe with negative emotions and feelings. If you are sad, be sad. You have a right to your feelings. Try to change your focus from the sad feelings by looking for something more positive to focus on. Be sad while you do something that you like to do. These activities will start creating feel-good hormones to replace the feel-bad hormones.

One way to start moving towards a more positive mindset is to develop an attitude of gratitude. Keep a gratitude journal. Developing a grateful mindset can be as simple as recording one to three things you are grateful for each day. You can also take regular deep dives into gratitude by journaling two to three times a week about a person, place, or thing in your life that you are grateful for. In this practice, you don't just list items you're grateful for. Instead, you explore why you're grateful for that thing, what qualities appeal to you, and how it makes you feel. This doesn't have to be time-consuming; five to ten minutes two to three times per week. Within a few weeks, you will start seeing and feeling the benefits of your gratitude practice in the form of a more positive voice in your head.

Confidence is also a great antidote to negative thinking. For the purposes of this chapter, here is a brief list of things you can try to help you build your confidence:

- Focus on your core values, strengths, wins, and learnings.
- Envision success but aim for mastery or the best you can, not perfection.
- Remember and relive your accomplishments with the use of self-affirmation.
- Practice power poses (stand in a superman pose) when you are feeling self-doubt.
- Be willing to take calculated risks, step out of your comfort zone, push boundaries.

Meditation or practicing mindfulness can also be helpful when your negative chatterbox has taken hold. You may find that your negative thoughts re-appear or interfere with your meditation. That's very normal. What you learn through meditation is how to work with your negative thoughts. With practice, you will learn to let the negative thoughts zip by like a tennis ball being volleyed around. You've likely already learned by now that beating them back with a mental tennis racquet volleys them back to you with a strong backhand. If you've tried mediation and have trouble sticking to it, that probably means that you just haven't found a form that suits you. I can't go into detail about all the different forms, but I encourage you to look up the work of Jon Kabat Zinn for some guidance about different forms of meditation.

Other ways to manage your negative chatterbox include:

- Volunteering—it helps to be helpful. You start feeling useful. It helps with your grateful mindset.
- Be social—get out in the world and talk to friends and family in person. Don't endlessly scroll news feeds.
- Develop a practice of self-care that includes tending to your physical, mental, spiritual, and even financial well-being.

You may be sitting there thinking about how stuck you are. You may understand the truth about change and fear, but you believe you are so stuck you can't move forward. I am here to tell you that you can and that your soul wants you to fly. I know taking that step into the unknown is scary. But I can also tell you it is exhilarating to start over to find new things to bring you joy. On the other side of fear of change, you can find your wonderland.

Rosalind is a life coach, co-host of the Relentless Transitions Podcast, and the Founder of Triskelion Transitions. She helps clients transform that scared little voice in their heads into a chorus of self-empowerment.

By the time she was 17 years old, she had moved towns and neighborhoods ten times. As a wife and mother, she moved nine times – seven of those moves were international moves. In her early 50's she started over as a divorcee. She learned from a young age how to transition to a new life. She knows how to start over and how to reinvent herself.

Her ideal clients are women in transition. Women who have reached a point in life where they ask themselves, "What's next?"

She is an accredited professional integral coach® and is certified to administer the EQi-2.0 and EQ360 assessments. She is a member of the International Coaching Federation.

Fun fact – as a child, she always wanted to learn to dance but didn't have the money to pay for lessons. As an adult, she has taken ballet, belly dancing, and ballroom dancing lessons. She still can't dance, but she has fun trying.

For more information about Rosalind, go to https://linktr.ee/TriskelionTransitions.

You can reach Rosalind at info@triskeliontransitions.com.

CHAPTER 12

THE YEAR OF DEATH

JOURNEYING THROUGH CHALLENGE AND LOSS TO LOVE AND LIGHT

Dr. Pamela J. Pine, PhD, MPH, MAIA, RCHES

This is a story I have created that draws on various elements, people, circumstances, and experiences. It presents a composite story and lessons learned from those components.

MY STORY

2020 presented us with confusion, isolation, loss, and sorrow—as if life doesn't present us with enough already.

Throughout our lives, we remember those days that we see through an unadulterated lens, like the day President Kennedy was shot. In fourth grade, the announcement came over the school PA system. We watched our teacher cry, right there, in front of the whole class! And like the day the Twin Towers collapsed, I was at work in Washington, DC. At first, I thought angrily, *I knew it would happen one day. Those darn air traffic controllers are overworked, and no one is addressing this!* Then another plane hit the second tower. I went out into the hallway, looked down at the other end, and saw the CEO of my company. He was a big man in his 60s, a tall, nice-looking man with gray hair and the comportment and body structure of most American men who successfully work their way into their 60s in white-collar jobs. Our eyes met and held each other's for what seemed like minutes but were likely seconds. We mirrored and held the same expression of confusion and fear on our faces, both thinking: *Oh my God.*

My life—perhaps everyone's life—is at least in part made up of these moments, many of them personal.

On Thursday, March 22, 2020, a feeling overcame me. I was standing in my yard at about 2 pm, taking a quick stroll to move my body a bit. The weather was normal for March in the DC area; everything was normal. The day started gray, preceded with some fog, and then moved into a hint of a drizzle. The temperature was in the lower 40s or so. A slight wind came from the south.

Suddenly, the sun peeked out at about 3 pm in the afternoon on this grayish day. I was wrapped in an unfamiliar feeling. My small frame felt warm and comforted; a love and peace came from my sister, Remi, living 2,877.1 miles away. There was no question where it came from. Her presence was solid, and the feeling resolute. Nearly as quickly, I shook myself, as one shakes off waking from an overpowering and disconcerting dream that's trying to tell you something too close to an uncomfortable truth: *This is not how my sister presents herself to me.* While she often told me, as an adult, that she loved me, it never felt tangible.

Remi was a highly sensitive baby, according to the letter I found from my father to my sister. It was written to her after my niece was born, in congratulations and to pass the baton. "Everything woke you up," the letter stated, "and nothing would calm you. You were a picky eater and colicky." When I was an adult, my aunt told me a story about when I was an infant. She said my mother came into the playroom to find Remi purposely pinching me to make me cry. My mother, this oh-so-against-any-corporal-punishment woman, smacked Remi to make her stop, so the story goes.

I'm three: "My sister picks her nose and eats it," I told a neighborhood kid, Linette, obtaining a little pleasure from confiding this disgusting secret to an older, five-year-old peer of my sister's. Remi, who hears about the fact that I've said this, drags me by my arm into our suburban home's garage. And, in front of that neighborhood kid, seemingly choosing at this so-young age, retaliation over mortification, smacks me as hard as she possibly can across my little face. I hear Linette at the end of the driveway—she audibly and sorrowfully says, "Ohhhh, don't do that." Shock. Fear. Humiliation. But no shame. That was my sister's to have and to hold.

I'm four, and my sister tells me there are toys in the cold, dusty, dark cellar of my grandparents' home out in rural Long Island, New York, where we're visiting for Thanksgiving dinner. I'm skeptical. Remi and my older cousin go down the cement stairs and stand right inside, reaffirming the presence of toys. I meander down the cement stairs distrustingly (I knew something was off). I get to the bottom when my sister and cousin run quickly past me up the stairs, shoving me inside and slamming the cellar door. I'm left in the pitch dark, utterly terrified and frantic, screaming as loud as I can until one of the grownups hears the shrill cries and lets me out.

I'm eight, and it's my birthday. My sister presents me with a huge box, nicely wrapped. I open it, and it's a little girl's dream, a giant green stuffed animal frog with a gold crown and smiling red mouth. Dino (as he looks like a dinosaur) becomes my favorite forevermore. I talk to him, and my words go to God. He stays with me until I leave for college.

I am ten, and it is my birthday again, and Remi presents me with a small wrapped box; I open it to find a gold birthstone ring. I can't figure it out in both these instances: *I know she hates me; why does she give me such great presents?*

I'm 15, and my sister is a cheerleader. Remi and I are on our front porch, waiting to enter the house where we have grown up after coming back from I-have-no-idea-where, and she's wearing those black and white saddle shoes—shitkickers, we sometimes called them. I walked past her and accidentally hit her nose with a box I was carrying. She turns around: "You stupid, fucking idiot," she says, and she hauls off and kicks me as hard as she can in my shin, with the *shit*kickers.

I'm 31, and I've been gone for a very long time, working far away. I'm visiting my family in California. Remi has invited me, and she's encouraging me to participate in her therapy session. I accept. *This could be interesting*, I think. We're sitting in the therapy session. At one point, Remi says, "The most deleterious thing that ever happened to me in my entire life was the birth of my sister." My eyebrows raise. *Wow*, I think. And, while, in retrospect, I wish I had it in me to look at her and say, "Gee, Remi, we really need to get to the bottom of this and help you work this out," I didn't feel safe enough to do that. So, instead, I turn to her, smile, shrug, and, with a sarcastic tone in the question presented, say, "Uh, sorry?"

I'm 38 and have surprised my sister for her birthday, having originally told her I couldn't come to her dance party because I'd be working. However, I got a flight out on Friday to be at the party the next night. It's 8:30 am, and I get up on the morning of the Saturday night party. After throwing on some sweats and washing up, I go around to the house of Remi's friend, Jane, to say hi and sit down for a cup of coffee. I've known Jane for a long time, since nearly when Remi met her in college in Boston, Massachusetts, when I visited.

After ten minutes, Remi arrives, and, with clenched fists on her hips, breathing like a bull in the arena ready to attack the red cape, she spits her words at me, "You stupid, lazy, selfish ass. Everyone is cleaning up for the party tonight, and you're sitting here, *chatting*!" I walk out. Remi is trailing behind me, saying, "You lazy, stupid, inconsiderate *bitch*!"

I stop and slowly turn around, and, since we're, give-or-take, half an inch from the same size as each other, I say, eye-to-eye, for the first but not the last time, "Remi, go *fuck* yourself." I have finally found my limit and my rage. And I turn around once more and walk off, repeatedly telling myself: *Don't let her do this, don't let her do this, walk around the block, and go back to Jane's house.*

That is what I do—I end up not going to the party. The next day, my brother-in-law, Dan, who towers over me and is visibly shaken and uncomfortable, catches me in the backyard and asks that I take a note of apology from Remi. "No," I say, "I'm not interested in her apologies, no more, I'm done."

"Just take it," he says. I take it, put it in a pocket, and never read it. I don't know what happened to it. Perhaps it got washed.

I'm 44 and have recently brought my one-and-a-half-year-old son home, who I adopted from Russia. I'm standing in the kitchen holding my son and hugging him, and I catch my daughter, who is three and a half years older than my son, out of the corner of my eye. Her little body is turned sideways to me, and her head is slightly turned in my direction, her eyes are turned to my son and me, and her mouth is pursed. She looks angry, disgusted, and jealous. And I say to her, "Leah, no matter how much I love this little boy, I will always, always, always love you. That will never, ever change. Not now. Not ever." Her entire expression changes. She is fine now. I knew what I was doing. I knew that no one ever said this to Remi.

I'm 63, and Remi calls and wants to nominate me for a major and prestigious award for my work. I say, "Thank you." She writes a glowing exposé of my work, and I get the award. She comes to the ceremony where hundreds of people are gathered to watch me get the award, and Remi tells me that she doesn't think I should thank her for nominating her in my speech. I'm astounded.

I'm 65 and preparing for a conference call with an international client, and the phone rings. "Do you have a few minutes?" asks Remi. "Only a very few right now. I'm preparing for a conference call in 20 minutes. What do you want to talk about?" I ask.

"Well, I can call back," says Remi.

"Why don't you just tell me what this is about so I can think about it and call you later?" I say.

"Well, did you call Loren because she's not speaking to me?" Remi says accusingly.

"Did I ever call Loren? Yes, I have called Loren. Did I ever call Loren to badmouth you? No, if that's where you're going." And now I'm upset, and I sound upset.

"What is this about?" I ask.

"Why do you sound so upset?" demands Remi, sarcastically and accusingly, once more.

"Because I'm preparing for a meeting that's now in ten minutes, and you have me going in some weird emotional direction, apparently accusing me of something outrageous out of the blue for no reason! I'll talk to you later. Goodbye." I hang up. I take my call and run errands. I have finally given up; I feel it in my entire being. Things will never change, and I'm now, indeed, done.

On the evening of March 22, 2020, I went about my day: working, running chores. That night, going to bed, I was shaking off the cold in the coldest room in the house, my bedroom. *There were never enough heat vents put in this room, damn it, and I'm always freezing in here,* I thought, as the temperature dropped to the upper 30s, with clouds and rain.

At about 3 pm on the March 23, I was driving to Lowe's Hardware, about 20 minutes away from my house, to pick up some wood to cover up and dress up the bottom of my bathroom closet door. It cracked and made my bathroom look shabby. *I'll get a piece of molding,* I thought, and pictured wood-gluing it on. *That will class it up.* I was halfway there, thinking, *I'll pick up some bulbs, too, and get ready for spring,* when my brother-in-law called with my sister's number coming up on the screen.

"Hi," I said with more than a hint of annoyance in my voice. "Jade," said my brother-in-law, "Can you talk?"

Realizing it was Dan, I perked up, "Sure. I'm driving, but my hands are free."

"Call me back when you're stopped at a place where you can sit and talk," he said.

"Well, okay, but I'm really okay to talk while I'm driving."

"Call me back," he said.

I drove the other ten minutes to Lowes, pulled into a parking place close to the store to avoid the chilly weather, and called Dan. "Are you parked?" said Dan.

"Yes, how are you?" I said cheerfully.

"Remi died yesterday. I found her near to death in the afternoon. It seemed like a death rattle, and I called the EMS, which started CPR and life-saving measures, which I knew Remi didn't want. They brought her to the hospital where she died a few hours later. She had been so sick for so long." He lowered his voice: "Ultimately, she left on her own terms."

Silence. The moment froze in time. My niece is desperately proclaiming something loud in the background, but it's just audible to me: "I asked her what she was going to do to get better? I just asked her that. I just asked. I didn't do anything." "It was not possible to bring her back," Dan went on. "She was too far gone."

"I knew something had changed," I said.

With a shiver, I told Dan about my sensation the previous day, just about the time when Remi was going from a conscious to an unconscious state. With her last willful act, Remi had sent the warmth and love to me that she always had as a part of what she'd felt and held but could never show or actualize.

That night, in my cold room, while I'm under the covers, my son, Mannis, comes in to talk to me and listen. I tell him stories of years of abuse and confusion. He stays for a while and just listens. "You have been through a lot," he says.

"Thank you for listening," I say.

After a while, he says, "Good night," and I say the same.

The night's temperatures fell into the lower 30s under the partly clear sky. I laid my head on my pillow, mused about my sister, and softly cried. I realize this is the first time in my adult life that I can fully feel sorry for her, her pain, struggles, and her lack of a sense of being okay. And now it's all done. There is no one to have to keep my guard up around. Now I miss her. I'm safe and warm under the heavy winter blankets, and I fall asleep.

THE TOOL

Dear Reader,

Of course, there is more to this story, and maybe someday it will be told. But this story is part of what brought me "home." I have become me; I'm close to who I was when I was born; that is what I believe. But it took at least half a lifetime to truly arrive. And I've discovered there are limits to everything, including patience and time.

I'm successful in ways most people would define that term, as was my sister. I continue to be active. I'm strong, creative, and bold. I'm nearly always content and sometimes even truly happy. And I believe there's more of that to come.

I have arrived with, perhaps, some words of wisdom and guidance for others—tools, if you will. Perhaps they'll be of interest and of use to you. Perhaps they'll help you navigate your lives.

First, it's not only what we come into the world with but also how we start it that gives us the seat from which we participate and watch things unfold. Living a life well-lived is, under the best of circumstances, complicated. Truly complicated. And difficult. Truly difficult. There are things you can do to help you steer.

Bring your children up so that they feel loved. Tell them this all the time, whether or not you think they're too young to understand. They will.

Stay attuned to the little and big needs of loved ones and others as you can. Try to understand as you can. Forgive as you can. We're not supermen or superwomen, and we cannot do it all; it takes an effort on others' parts, but we can do our share. Tell people how you feel. See if you can help them as well as yourself. Navigate through it. If you can do it calmly, that's best, so they can best hear you.

However, don't let yourself be abused. Abuse compounds itself, and it becomes a habit. Draw those lines in the sand. Do it earlier rather than later if you can.

But do it. Whether they are lovers, friends, bosses, coworkers, or family members, people have no right to abuse you. Stand up for yourself. Get the help you need if you cannot do it yourself. Leave obviously harmful situations.

Be bold. Take calculated risks. These will help you work through the difficult beginnings and the rocks or boulders along the way.

Find out who you are and hold onto it because it's going to be quite a ride any way you cut it.

Dr. Pamela J. Pine grew up in suburban New Jersey and has lived in semi-rural Maryland from the late 1980s after returning from nearly a decade working overseas. She has been an international public health, development, and communication professional since the late 1970s concentrating on enhancing the lives of the poor and otherwise underserved groups, and an artist. Pamela has worked throughout the world from Latin America to Oceania on some of the world's most difficult issues, including Hansen's Disease (leprosy), HIV, tropical diseases, childhood immunization programs, and maternal and child health. She speaks Arabic and French. Pamela is a professor of public health and an international health consultant. Since 2000, she's been the Founder and Director of an international program focused on preventing, treating, and mitigating child sexual abuse (CSA) and other adverse childhood experiences (ACEs). She developed and tested a comprehensive CSA/ACEs prevention/ mitigation modeled by local presence, adaptable for any country. She is an expert in CSA and trauma prevention/ mitigation and is called upon regularly by the media to provide authoritative input. She was honored in 2017 with a Lifetime Achievement Award in Advocacy from the Institute on Violence, Abuse, and Trauma (IVAT) in San Diego, CA. Pamela is on the National Partnership to End Interpersonal Violence Board, an advisor to IVAT, and on the Advisory Board of the Clinical and Counseling Psychology Review, Lahore, Pakistan. Pamela's Ph.D. is from UMD; her MPH from Johns Hopkins Bloomberg School of Public Health; and her International Affairs Degree from Ohio University. Given a childhood interest in art and ongoing training at Eastman School of Music and Cornell University, she continues to sing, paint, and write and is a published author. In her free time, Pamela spends time with family and friends, gardens, travels, reads, and exercises.

Connect with her on the following sites:

Email: pamelajpine@gmail.com

Website: https://www.drpamelajpine.com

LinkedIn: https://www.linkedin.com/in/pamela-j-pine-3123b78/

Twitter: https://twitter.com/DrPamelaJPine1

CHAPTER 13

THE KEY TO YOUR DREAM LIFE

HOW TO USE EMOTIONS FOR DAILY CLARITY

Aura E. Martinez

MY STORY

Damn, did my 30s shake me hard.

I landed in Rome. I'm in a spacious room that feels more like an apartment than a hotel. The room has a living room with a TV, a comfortable sofa, and a window where sunlight shines directly in. The bedroom is equally spacious, with a bed that is not too hard and not too soft, just right for my body.

I have every reason to feel happy and fortunate. For God's sakes, I am in Rome! I just had the privilege to walk down the streets of Rome to head to the supermarket and get some groceries to take back to the U.S., and now I have 24 hours all to myself in one of the most beautiful cities in the world.

Yet, here I am, unhappy for some reason. I didn't understand why; I just knew I was not happy. I travel the world for a living, yet, it wasn't enough. I have the luxury to travel the world even on my days off, but that didn't fulfill me. I made good money; however, it wasn't about the money for me.

What is wrong with me? I thought. *Is this just it when it comes to life? Just wake up, do what you're supposed to do, and then rinse and repeat? If this is it, then where is the real joy of life?*

I tried so hard to suppress the frustration and unhappiness growing within me, but it just got louder and louder.

"Massimiliano, I don't know why but I feel like I'm meant to be doing either something else or something more. I don't know, but something needs to change." I expressed this to a friend of mine in Rome.

Walking down Fontana Di Trevi, marveled and at the same time perplexed at how you could be "living a great life" and your inner being not feel like that is the case, I couldn't help but wonder, *how does one get themselves to this point in life?*

Another freaking day doing the same ol' same ol.' This crossed my mind every damn morning. This isn't the real me! This is not how I truly think, this is not who I am at my core, but I couldn't seem to shake what was going on within me.

I finally reached a weight at 30 that I was in my teenage years. I traveled to places I could only dream of visiting. Every week I was in my favorite country in the world, had both parents alive, basically, all the things that one would need to consider themselves lucky. I felt so far from feeling lucky.

I didn't know then that this was the beginning of a series of events that would crack my shell open to becoming the person I am.

Me: "Something to drink?"

Passenger: "Huh?"

Me: "Something to drink?"

Passenger: "What did you say?"

I placed my hand over my ears with my fingers making a C shape and moved my hands out to indicate for him to remove his headphones.

You would hear me if you just removed your headphones; I couldn't help thinking.

Me: "Something to drink?"

I normally wouldn't be this annoyed, but I couldn't help myself. Of course, I hid what I thought and felt, but was I annoyed!

The following months were met with more frustration and confusion. *Seriously, how can I shake what I'm feeling? Could it be that this is not the job I'm supposed to be doing after all? Could it be that I need to go back to school and change careers? God, please, help me because I can't stand this feeling anymore!*

What made everything so confusing was that traveling is something that I so love, and I knew I didn't see myself doing nine-to-five anything. I felt I didn't know how to piece together the pieces of the puzzle of me and my life, especially being someone good at several things.

What occurred during several flights just amazed me to the core, and I knew it had to be God.

"You seem like someone that we have so much to learn from."

Huh? Where did that come from? I couldn't believe it. A passenger, out of the blue, who didn't even know me—but clearly she'd been observing me throughout the flight—said that to me.

"You light this whole cabin with your presence."

Omggggg! Did that passenger just say that to me?!

"Thank you, thank you so much," I replied.

"May I speak to you for just a minute? What would you like to do in life? Because someone like you could be the ambassador of the United States if you wanted to."

Okay, at this point, I knew this wasn't a coincidence. These are three different flights, none of these passengers knew each other, and I just knew I couldn't ignore any of this.

From that point on, I decided to remain open to what the Universe had in store for me. I stayed aware of the clues it was giving me. For the first time, I decided to lean into my frustration.

The decision to lean into my frustration led to a curiosity. My frustration was a no longer a bother. If anything, my frustration fascinated me.

It's a new day kind of thinking led to thoughts of, *I'm curious what this day has in store for me*, which led me to enjoy every day. And it was then that I understood that my frustration was there for me, beckoning me inward. And inward I went.

You're meant to be doing more, apart from what you're currently doing. That was the voice I heard one morning in the middle of meditating. I knew that was exactly where my frustration stemmed from.

Whew, what a relief to know that it's not that I am frustrated with my job. It's that my soul wants more. My soul doesn't mind what I'm doing now. It loves what it's doing, and it longs for so much more.

"Alrighty then. So much more it is!"

Oooo, acting classes sounds interesting. Now, this made no sense to me whatsoever, but I reached a point where I was just curious to see what was in store for me. The acting was not what I wanted to do, but boy did I learn some valuable lessons.

Cooking sure is fun. And off I went cooking my heart out. I lost lots of weight in the process and learned to meal prep and carry my food everywhere.

Some years passed by, and here I am, sitting in the hospital's waiting area at one of my father's many appointments. I already knew the wait would be long, so I made sure to pack my food, have a good book with me, and a notebook in case inspiration did strike. And boy, did inspiration strike!

As I'm eating my strawberries with cashews, all of a sudden, a voice rushes within me: *Wellness coach.*

That's it! That resonates with me! I heard my calling!

The rest is history, leading me to this point right now, as I write this chapter.

How often do you brush underneath the rug what you feel, thinking it has no importance? How many times do you judge and shame yourself for how you feel? Have you found yourself, or do you find yourself anesthetizing what's going on within with food, drinks, gambling, etc.? And how many times have you been so anxious to figure certain things out in your life to the point that you're in a constant state of frustration?

All this is poison for your soul. Anything poisonous for the soul will eventually infect your mind, emotions, physical body, actions, and everything else externally. Also, remaining in a state of anxiousness keeps you away from the answers you're looking for.

I share this story with you because we often make ourselves wrong for how we feel. I would dare to say we do this many times. Every time we do, we atrophy the trust muscle. We chip away from our confidence in trusting ourselves.

One of the biggest mistakes we make as human beings is to brush what goes on inside underneath the rug, as if it's just a phase or something of no importance. When we do this, we amputate a big part of us, and we paralyze our soul, mind, and life because we don't allow ourselves to access the infinite wisdom that exists within us.

Although you are not your emotions, your emotions are a part of you. They're information from your soul, guiding you to your next step in life.

There is a big difference between you being your emotions and your emotions being a part of you. The first is acting out how you're feeling, thereby identifying yourself as that emotion. When the feeling you're living from is one that only spirals you down, this is when that emotion can become a liability. When it's the latter, you understand your feelings are there to serve you, not hurt you.

To the degree you're frustrated in any area of your life, whether that's work, your love life, your weight, or anything for that matter, there is a disconnect between what you're experiencing in your outer world and your true essence, which is your soul. It then becomes your job to understand what that disconnect is. And what a beautiful job this is.

THE TOOL

For this, *you* are the primary tool. You will also need some quiet time, a pen and paper or a recorder.

1. To figure out what that disconnect is, you first must remove that situation/circumstance or person as the reason for what you're feeling, be it work, love life, etc. As long as you're pointing the finger to something outside of you for why you feel what you feel–even if that may be the actual reason why you find yourself where you are– you'll never truly get to the deeper why.

2. After you have done this, sit with the emotion you're experiencing at this moment. Give yourself some quiet time where you will not be disturbed by anything or anyone. The purpose of this is for you to be in touch with yourself and get the answers you need. As you are giving yourself this quiet time, ask that feeling some questions and wait to see what answers you receive. Some of the questions you can ask that emotion are:

Why do you feel this way?

What do you need from me?

What do you wish to experience right now?

Depending on the answers you get, you can ask it further questions. The point is to ask all the questions necessary to get to the root cause of what you are experiencing.

3. Make sure that you're recording your answers. Write them down, or if you're not much of a writer, record yourself saying the answers you receive. Relying on your memory for this won't help, and it will be of great use for you to go back to what you wrote or recorded later when you're feeling a bit different.

4. As you receive your answers, make sure not to judge them. Just remain curious. Curiosity is the start of a transformation. Also, be willing to allow things to get messy. At first, things may not seem to make sense. What you feel guided to do may not seem to have any relevance for your current life, and certain things may seem crazy to do. Still lean in because one thing leads to the next and the next.

   "You don't need to see the whole staircase, just take the first step." as Dr. Martin Luther King used to say. This is what will be required of you if you are to live your dream life.

5. Don't get disappointed if you do not get the answers you are looking for right away. Just remain open and be patient. I need to emphasize this because when you get anxious to know the answers, you get yourself further away from the wisdom you are seeking. Instead, relax in the knowledge that the answer will come to you at the right moment.

6. Pay attention to the things around you that seem like coincidences. The Universe has a way of communicating the very things we need to hear and know. Follow the breadcrumbs. As you pay attention to the things around you, pay attention to what occurs within you. Pay attention to what you feel led to do, even if it doesn't make any sense to you.

7. Enjoy yourself along the way. This is the key to truly unlocking the door of your wisdom because when you enjoy and delight yourself in the journey, even when it doesn't make any sense, the pieces of the puzzle start coming together.

A life full of purpose requires you to be in touch with yourself, and it means embracing all your emotions without making them wrong. None of your emotions are wrong or bad. All emotions are meant to work in your favor. What makes any emotion a negative one is how you handle it, meaning if you decide to live from that emotion rather than understanding its message and doing something positive with its message.

There is so much wisdom within you, more than you can imagine. It's a matter of trusting your wisdom and what's within you, utilizing your emotions as your guiding system, and any input you receive from the outside world. You consult first with your inner being to see if it resonates.

So, this story has several lessons:

1. At times what we think is the reason for our frustration, misery, or anger isn't the source of that emotion.

2. Negative emotions grow louder when you ignore them, just like a child cries louder when ignored to get your attention.

3. The Universe is always providing you with signs, and it's up to you to pay attention.

4. There is no such thing as coincidences, so pay to what appears to be random things.

5. Curiosity soothes any bothersome emotion you may feel.

6. Your emotions are your guiding system.

7. What may annoy you may not be the real cause for the annoyance, dig deep within to find the real reason.

Your dream life requires you to start paying attention to what is going on in your inner world and to use your emotions because they are the key to your dream life and living on purpose.

Aura E. Martinez is a Self-Discovery & Empowerment Coach, helping women gain total clarity in their purpose so they can wake up to a life of daily fulfillment & certainty. She is the creator of Aura Blueprint™ and founder of Live to the Max™/Viva al máximo™. She is also the author of the book *Creating a Lifetime of Wellness: Start Having the Life You Deserve*, and the book has been seen in *Spirituality & Health* magazine, *Psychology Today*, and *Natural Awakenings NYC edition* magazine. Sign up for your weekly dose of wellness & empowerment via her site: www.auraemartinez.com

CHAPTER 14

ONE PART OF YOU

HERE TO STAY

Meilin Ehlke, MLA

MY STORY

The distinct sound of packing tape being torn off its roll greeted me from behind the door as I fiddled around to push my key into the lock. I felt glad to have made it home this quickly as I heard the movers busy packing up our belongings.

I noticed my arm becoming sore from scrubbing away at the last paint on the walls in my atelier. I passed the white glove test before handing over the keys to my art studio to my landlord. Though at the same time relieved, melancholy crept up, as I remembered being in awe the first time I stepped into this morning sun-filled room overlooking the forest. How happy I was, finding my atelier just as I had envisioned, within a short walk away from my son's outdoor kindergarten nestled close to the river in an environment considered a haven of inspiration for any artist.

Wow, I am closing a chapter in my life again, just two years after arriving here in Munich. When does it end? I had just started putting my roots into this area. I had, at last, become creative again and finished some fantastic paintings. Finally, I have enough pieces to exhibit at an art gallery. All these thoughts flashed through my head as I pushed the door open and entered the hallway of our almost empty apartment.

My handbag only touched the ground a few seconds when the crew leader turned the corner, greeting me in a mumble, "Good morning, Mrs. Ehlke." Moving my tray filled with four coffees in his direction, I replied with still a tint of melancholy in my voice, "Good morning. Coffee?" With an appreciating nod, he reached for a cup. As he suddenly hesitated, I noticed his body slouch and rebuild itself in an instant before he informed me, "Our truck burned down."

"That's a joke!" I replied. I heard him say it but couldn't grasp it, thinking *he was playing with me.*

'No! Our truck burned down on the way home to Nuernberg yesterday," he reiterated.

We had such a great conversation yesterday as we wrapped up my art pieces. He can't be serious, I thought in disbelief.

Yesterday, first thing, I took the crew down with me to the kindergarten to pack up the studio first, so one thing would be done and out of my mind. *Why did I do that?*

Still, dumbfounded, I stood there looking at him, trying to put it all together. When I did not attempt to move or say anything, he said, "Wait," and disappeared into the living room. I followed him into the living room, where he stood scrolling through his cellphone. I could feel the other two men gazing at me intensely.

"Everything burned on the autobahn. It was even on the radio." One of them explained as he gently took the coffee tray off my hand and placed it on the couch table.

The moment the small cellphone screen was held in front of my eyes, I saw what looked exactly like a typical child's picture, a square for the back of the moving van and two vertical black bars as tires all covered by one huge yellow-orange flame. But this was not a painting of a child; this was the truck I had seen yesterday drive off with all my art in it, now on fire. Years of collecting material, experimental and exhibit pieces, gifts, and all memories of my artist's life just vanished into smoke before my eyes. I stared at his video; it was surreal but also so real.

As I grasped what was happening, the first words out of my mouth were, "There must be a reason for this to happen?" The crew leader looked at me in disbelief in response to my indifferent expression. Those words may have been channeled as they reflected my shamanic way of dealing with the situation. Slowly I walked out onto the balcony and bathed in the faint spring sun rays to warm my body. *Why did this happen? I don't even know why?* Silently in the fresh air, I waited until my tears could run down my cheeks.

The next morning, when I greeted the movers in our new home as they brought in boxes, I noticed that they were still missing the vigor of the day I met them. *The shock of having physically experienced the explosion was still in their bones. They must be glad to have safely made it out of the truck before the flames turned everything into coal.* The crew leader pulled me out of my thoughts and asked me, "Please, write down all items burned with the truck on Monday. I need the list before we leave." *I must do this, even though I had to delegate where to put all the boxes in the house?* I groaned, contemplating the vastness of the task, and sat down obediently to do what I was told. The worst thing was my designated art room would house no boxes.

I wrote down what I could remember between saying, "Upstairs" or "Downstairs," to the movers as they passed me with furnishings or boxes. There were paintbrushes, oil tubes, papers, tables, canvases, frames, finished art pieces of all sizes, and much more. Poking on my own wound drained my energy, trying to remember it all.

Once everyone left, I stood in the room that should have housed all of my art. I envisioned doing healing art and energy art to impact, transform, and heal the world. All these visions dissolved into the vapor of nothingness.

Luckily, a few weeks later, my husband would find the professionally made packing list from our overseas move back to Germany of all my art supplies. That ensured the insurance reimbursement. I thank spirit so often for that, even though it was a drop in the bucket for my mental state.

The following summer, I lay in the sun around noon, stretched out on the grass, my palms touching the ground and feeling the earth below me. I sensed how it carries me, holds me up, or in a way, envelops me—from the top, letting the warm sun rays penetrate my body so that I could feel the tingle created by the heat. In a way, it was restructuring, reprogramming, and revitalizing me. I needed to feel alive and was longing for support. I was lost in the world of questions, or was I. *Who am I? What should I do now? What is my purpose? Why now? Why me? Did I want this? Isn't art a part of me anymore?*

Somehow, as often in my life, I get or am pushed back on my feet. Not having touched a paintbrush since the fire, I was attracted to it one spring day. While I roamed an alternative gift store, I found brilliant colored paint bottles. My eyes were fascinated by the painting materials. Nothing can smother an embodied divine gift. My research revealed that it was watercolors made from plant pigments. I ordered some with the anticipation of experimenting for the first time with plant pigments, especially because my intention, while deepened during my shamanic studies, was to neglect synthetic materials in my life. I began to aim toward everything I use in my home and work to be medicine for myself and others.

On my search for natural brushes, I stumbled over handmade paper cards in a new art store I scouted. They were five by five centimeters and texturized. It all came together again. I wanted to test my new supplies with enthusiasm as I felt the creation thirst rekindled. Though I just couldn't move into action.

It took almost a year and the gentle nudge of my Swiss friend to insert the missing puzzle piece. I was invited to keep her company during an esoteric trade show back in Munich, and I brought along my paint box in case I had time on my hands. I did. Sitting in the corner of her booth, I dipped the brush into the liquid and painted a symbol. My hand just did it. No thoughts guided it.

The moment I laid the tiny piece of paper to dry, a woman came by to look at it.

"Oh, how beautiful!" she remarked, "What is it?"

"It is an energy painting." Those were the words that just came out of my mouth.

She placed the paper on her heart. Stunned, she felt its energy warm her heart, so I decided to gift the drawing to her.

I was back in the game. *Yippee.* A different game, though. Simpler. Faster. Softer. A new style and twist awoke within me. I loved myself, this reborn artist, and I still do. You can take art from me, but you can't take the art out of me.

THE TOOL

Feel part of it all.

We are part of all that exists on this beautiful blue planet. But, so often, we neglect to invite nature, animals, and people to be there for us when we need them. You are invited to acknowledge your belonging to the all and to feel like one whenever you long for feeling supported and for your spirit to be lifted again.

You are invited to walk out into nature when you desire to fill up your body with vital bioenergy. As you do, breathe in the fresh air. Look around to familiarize yourself with the landscape surrounding you. Gaze far out into the blue sky and notice the clouds. Greet the sun and the moon and the stars.

Look for an environment where you feel comfortable and save enough to rest for a while. Maybe on a rock or against a tree, or you can choose to lie on the ground.

Make yourself comfortable. Take in a breath and exhale. Shift your body to make yourself more comfortable. Become aware of what parts of you are touching what you are resting on. Observe your breathing rhythm.

Sense the temperature below and above you. The heat. The warmth. The hot. The cold. The cool. The icy.

Taste the air. The salt. The humidity. The wetness. The dryness.

Feel the wind. Be aware of the different textures and materials touching your body. The smooth. The rough. The prickly. The fuzzy. The slimy. Observe your breathing rhythm.

Notice yourself becoming one with the earth below. Notice what you are touching is becoming one with you. You are exchanging information. You are learning from each other. You are teaching each other.

Acknowledge what is below you even further down. The bacteria. The fungi. The sand. The leaves. The stones. The bark. The worms. Observe your breathing rhythm.

Sense the vibration, movement, shaking, tremble, rumble below you. Listen to the rhythm of the materials below.

Listen to your body's fluids. Observe your breathing rhythm.

Hear the leaves rustle in the wind, and the birds sing as they soar—the laughter of children and the dogs and seals that bark. Hear the humans talk—the bees buzz, the clams clap, and the movement of the waves.

Smell the soil. The sand. The grass. The flower. The snow. The stone. The salt in the air. Observe your breathing rhythm.

Sense the material left of you. The trees. The scrub. The mountain. The lake. The road. The house. The cliff. The dune. The flower.

Hear what exists to the right of you. The pouncing cat. The running water. The cracking branches. The falling fruits. Observe your breathing rhythm.

Feel your body's pressure points upon the materials you have been sitting, standing, or lying on. They hurt. They numbed. They merged. They tingle. They stiffen. They cramped. They softened.

Observe your breath. Observe your expansion. Observe your lightness. Observe you as oneness. Observe being an integral part of all.

Notice what direction was the easiest for you to sense. Which direction was the most difficult? Where did your body tighten? When did your breathing break its rhythm? Where did your body hurt?

What senses were you more aware of? Hearing. Seeing. Smelling. Tasting. Touching.

Do this awareness exercise once more with closed eyes. What is more pleasant for you? Feel free to follow your own script. Play with it. Become creative while interacting with your chosen environment. The rewards are grand. Did you notice you are never alone?

Meilin Ehlke is the go-to shamanic channeler for writers, spiritual creatives, and enlightened entrepreneurs to experience magical moments to reveal the beauty in all things: earth wisdom, universal language, and knowledge of the unending realities.

As a world-renowned artist and healer, Meilin reaches a global audience on her podcast 'Moving To Oneness', radio shows, and peace events. For seven years and over 400 episodes, Meilin has confidently led hundreds of thousands to reconnect to their wisdom, allowing her audience to embody themselves fully, wake up to what is possible, and listen to their inner guidance.

Meilin resides in a small village outside of Nürnberg, Germany. She lived as a student and landscape architect in the United States for two decades before she was called back to her native land to activate sacred sites in the heart of Europe (and beyond).

Over the past 15 years, Meilin has been known as an energy art medium, a gateway guide for you to grow with intention, embody your wisdom, bloom into your beauty, and flourish into your true self.

Being in the sacred rhythm of life, she feels it's vitally important to fully express your message radiantly from the inside out and stand in your grandness.

Meilin will lead you on a manifesting journey before materializing your vision. Her process will spiral you through singing, dancing, channeling, and more so that you can stand in your full power, potential, and intention, gracefully dissolving the borders of your beliefs and sharp corners of the roles you play every day.

Meilin welcomes you to her website, www.meilinehlke.com, and loves to hear from you via email info@meilinehlke.com or on the major social platforms under Meilin Ehlke.

CHAPTER 15

WITHOUT A POWERFUL COMMUNITY, THERE IS NO SUCCESS

3 KEY STEPS TO BUILD A LIFETIME OF WEALTH BY CREATING A COMMUNITY IN ALL PARTS OF YOUR LIFE

Melinda Holmes, CHC

MY STORY

"Huuuuuuh! Huuuuuh! Huh! It was the rhythm of my breath. You couldn't tell me someone didn't slam a load of bricks on my chest. The January cold air invaded my lungs. This was how my train commute from work ended every night, traveling from New York City to New Jersey that month.

I woke up every morning thinking, *did the Universe make a mistake?* The air greeted me with a cold breeze hitting my nose. The darkness outside stared at me and did not welcome me into the morning. I pounded on the snooze button, turned over into my bed of clouds, snuggled back in as if my bed were my partner, comforting me, feeling safe and warm. *How would I get my body out of bed feeling like I weighed a ton?* The reminder of the long walks going from train to train and trekking to my office with marathon Manhattan blocks tried to encourage me to stay home.

I can't do this today. I just can't! By some miracle, I would. After getting ready, I scrambled for my keys, threw my coat on, and did my famous ninja move out the door, fumbling with the keys to lock the door. Block after block, I huffed and puffed, trying to catch my breath. *Why the heck am I drenched in sweat, and is it 40 degrees outside?*

After I got sardined on the train, dragging my now thin body to walk, I was rewarded with the wondrous entry into work. With no smile on my face, I said, "Good morning." Attempting to start a normal day with no appetite, I forced myself to eat, but the food was yelling at me inside my belly. A morning of nausea, the imposter of seasickness would rock my stomach back and forth over and over again.

The best part—moments of anger as they would rapidly trigger me appearing out of nowhere. It could be a scent that hit my nose and linger around like an unwelcome house guest, a sound or screech of someone's voice. *Oh no, Melinda girl, it is too damn early for menopause!* I was about to go over the edge and snap, but I remember I needed this job.

I noticed the blank stares at me—the raised eyebrows. I knew something was not right with my body. I wasn't ready to know until the final straw. I remember the night. I thought it would be my last. Walking up the hill from the train felt like climbing Mount Everest; the chest pain hit me like a bullet. My chest felt like a knot getting tied over and over again. I was in the street leaning against a stranger's fence for at least ten minutes; after the pain left, I sighed, I was given a second chance in life.

Melinda, take your butt to the doctor!

The next day I went. "Next!" The medical clerk called me up.

"Ma'am, do you have an appointment?" She tapped on the desk, waiting for an answer.

"No, I called this morning, and they said I can come in, and I. . ."

Before I could finish, she slammed the clipboard on the counter, "Please fill this out. Front and back, please."

I wish she would have said, "Everything's going to be alright, Sis. Don't you worry, we got you."

Back then, I didn't reach out to friends or family to tell them how bad it was. I was always like; *I will just figure it out myself.* I was always struggling and making it harder than it was. Too proud, or too ashamed to admit I made a mistake. I was blessed with great family and friends but still failed to reach out for support. Deep down inside, that's what I needed at that very moment.

I created a laundry list of what I was experiencing. The medical assistant listened and wrote down all of my symptoms.

"Oh sweetie, it sounds like you have anxiety."

"Oh yeah, you think it's anxiety?"

"Maybe. . .but the doctor will be in soon to see what could be the issue, and then we will take some blood."

"Okay. . .thanks."

My Doctor entered with her concrete poise and confidence. I went to her for years because of her great, patient service, and she was attentive. She cared for her patients and always gave helpful advice. After restarting my list of symptoms to the doctor, she checked my vitals. "Huh?" She looked at me, took a few steps back without taking her eyes off of me.

"Oh yes, doctor, look what happens when I hold my phone." My hands shook like an earthquake rattling a vase on a bookshelf about to tumble down.

"Hmmmmm?" She paused for a few moments. I am going to send you to the lab for bloodwork. "I hope it's not your thyroid."

"Oh, my thyroid. Oh, okay." I didn't think much of it until my cell phone rang with my disco-funk style ringtone a few days later. I figured it was just anxiety from the domino effect of losing four loved ones in 2019, along with the stress of the job and not eating right consistently.

I just needed another herbal cleanse.

"Hello."

"Hi, Melinda, this is the doctor's office. Your thyroid levels are high, so the doctor wants you to make an appointment with the endocrinologist. She sent a prescription to your pharmacy. Start taking the medication right away."

"Oh, okay, alright. Thanks."

I texted my mentor to tell her. She mentored me for years when I was getting certified to be a wellness coach. After texting, she called me back right away.

"Hey Dr. Lajoyce Brookshire, how are you?"

"I'm good. What are they saying about your thyroid?"

"They said it's high."

"I don't like your levels showing up in your blood work. I don't like it."

My ears were glued to everything she said. She gave me a list of supplements to take, what to eat and drink for two weeks, and instructed me to go back and test again. I decided to follow her instructions instead of taking the prescribed medicine. My body was crying out to me, and it was time to go back to my roots and start paying attention.

This was when the journey started; I thought I knew what was all wrong about my life and holding me back in business, and why my body was screaming at me.

Two weeks later, I returned to my doctor's office. I was excited because, in just two weeks, I felt 90% better with Dr. Lajoyce Brookshire's direction. The doctor entered. I felt the wind from her body as she entered the examiner's room. Her face was red, and her breathing was off.

"How are you? I called the endocrinologist only to hear you haven't made an appointment. Melinda, this is very dangerous; you have to see him right away."

"When did you start the medication?" She asked.

"Well, I wanted to share with you my progress. I have been eating better and taking some great supplements, and I feel so much better."

"And what about the medication?"

"I'm not taking the medication."

Her mouth dropped open. She plopped her hands to her side, making a loud pop sound as her hand hit her thighs without a breath shaking her head, staring me right in the eye.

"You haven't started the medication yet? You probably have Graves's Disease. Melinda, you can have a thyroid storm; you can die. I recommend you go to the hospital."

I sighed to myself. I felt like she was overacting. "I have a trip already planned for my birthday this February. I will just take the medication while I'm there to be safe."

"With everything going on with you and this new virus, they're probably going to cancel your trip anyway."

I just shook my head and shrugged at this point. I knew she was a caring doctor, I knew she meant well and was doing her job, but I did not panic. I didn't go with her recommendation. I knew my body could heal. A few days later, I packed my bags and set off on my adventure.

THE ADVENTURE

I would know no one at this retreat. It was part of my adventure. I arrived on a bright clear day in Portland, Jamaica, in the untouched countryside of the beautiful island. The air was cleansing, the sound of the waves crashing against my heart, and the beauty of the natural gift of colors from the ocean, earth, and sky was so vivid I wanted to cry. I was where I needed to be during this time in my life.

As the cab pulled up to the yoga community after four hours of curves, twists, and turns on the adventurous roads, I had butterflies and was getting anxious at the meeting and the being around new people. The staff had beautiful smiles. The guests at the retreat warmed me up with their beautiful words. We all came from different parts of the world, different ages, and walks of life, but one thing we all shared and had in common was that we were looking to take our lives to the next level for the next chapter of our lives. I don't think we realized it at the time, but we wanted a true community. The love of my Yoga teacher embraced me. She was so patient with me as I learned for the first time all about Yoga. I knew I could end up in the downward facing dog if all else failed.

I didn't realize how much I had already healed during the six-day retreat. It wasn't until over a year later that it was clear to me that the energetic connection and power of sharing with those powerful women helped me through my healing journey.

A year after the retreat, I lost touch with the ladies. I had a few failed professional and personal relationships from 2020 to 2021. I also had a failed business plan and a lack of consistency on my part. I thought it was a failure, but today I know it wasn't. It was time to be truly honest with myself. It was 2021, and I was still riding on the same roller coaster of uncertainty about my health, life plans, my business, and it was due to a lack of consistency. *Melinda, you are trying to heal alone. You need just to do and stop saying what you intend to do!* I rarely reached out for help; I chose to do it alone. I needed to reach out for help. I needed support this time around.

GETTING WITH THE PROGRAM

I heard about a group program that helps people like myself heal from autoimmune diseases, mental disorders, and other health challenges. The program was structured well with a great online system. Every morning we were greeted with an insightful email along with our daily module to be completed by the end of each day. There was great client support via email. The best part was the weekly calls on Zoom, where we were allowed to connect and meet members of the community. We shared our stories, struggles, tears, and our laughs. I will never forget one of the members who cried during one session because she didn't get support from her family or friends. They made her feel like a failure, and she didn't know how she would cope. With a trembling voice, she said, "I don't know if I'm good enough."

The online community sent out so much love during the chat and reached out to her in private chats. I sank into my chair. *I know exactly how you feel, Katie.* To think I thought I could heal alone. I knew I needed this community more than the food guidelines I religiously followed, more than the thousands of supplements I took, more than the Yoga and meditation I did at 5 a.m. every morning. I needed the power of "we" and not "just me." I needed a powerful and strong community.

About a month after completing the 45-day program, I went for my routine bloodwork. When I got the results, all I could do was lift my voice, "Aaah! Aaah! Woo! Yes!" I jumped up and down, not caring if my neighbors thought I had lost my mind. My thyroid levels improved. The numbers dropped significantly. Food and lifestyle are the sources, but the community was where the magic happens to synchronize all the radical changes I made in my life.

This is why today, as I partner with small businesses on how to create a concierge VIP client experience to increase profits and retain customers they already have, I help them implement a strong community culture into their business model.

It's not just for business; it's for personal life as well. It's impossible to separate your personal life and your business. No matter how much you try, one will pour into the other in some type of way.

There are three parts of building a strong and powerful community in your personal and business life, which create success.

THE COMMUNITY

After farm hopping on Halloween on the rural side of New Jersey one fall with one of my close friends, we found this cozy restaurant to eat at. I requested if they could substitute certain foods that weren't best for my healing journey with my health goals.

"Hi, ma'am, instead of fried chicken fingers, could I please have it grilled with the Brussel sprouts and a side of baked sweet potato?"

"Absolutely, not a problem." Moments later, the owner came out to greet my friend and me at our table and with a smirk on his face, "Which one of you ladies changed your order." I admitted with pride, "Yes, that would be me." My friend and I giggled.

Snapping his head back, "Wow, that is exactly how I ask for the same meal to be prepared, so I had to come out to see who it was." We had a great conversation about the restaurant. He shared how he and his wife ran the restaurant, and despite the pandemic, they did extremely well. Excitement shined through his eyes, his smile glowed. He loved his town and his community of customers, and he took care of them. From our first encounter with him, it was no surprise that he lived a life with a powerful community. It saved his business in an industry that struggled during the pandemic.

The next year, I partnered with him and planned a cooking contest event for his community with his marketing team, which created more engagement and involved his customers, which enhanced the experience he had already established. This event created more of a buzz for his business, welcomed more customers, and impressed those already in his community. It increased retention and engagement in his community, and together we created a great experience.

Creating a strong and powerful community starts at home. The first part is the power of connection and community with family, friends, and your partner. It's about strategically creating a support system to support you during the challenges and roadblocks. Make sure you are not the smartest one in your community. It would help if you had a few from your team who have already walked the path where you are striving to go. This is the heartbeat.

The second part is building a community of a dream team. These are your partnerships, business mentors, colleagues, experts, a personal or virtual assistant who knows how to accomplish the tasks you don't have the expertise in, time, or interest in doing it.

These two parts are the foundation to provide all you need to create a successful community for your customers. Building a community for your customers is based on what they exactly want and need. Our goal is to create and develop a community with a following that shares a common goal or desire. It creates raving fans, a place they belong, and a second home that supports them through their journey.

It can be a virtual or in-person event such as a retreat, a monthly Q&A session, a weekly support session, a monthly celebration night. These examples are solely the shell, the place your community meets, but the secret sauce to building a strong, powerful, unstoppable community is discovering what the glue is that holds everyone together. You will see your retention rates increase, and future clients will be drawn to you by referrals and word of mouth. It will sum up to more profits and longevity of success in your business. Most of all, like Mike, who owns the restaurant, it was part of his life's fulfillment.

THE TOOL

Step 1: To get started on building your life community, take a sheet of paper and make three columns. Write the first names that come to mind which you see fit into one of the three parts of your community whether you know them at this moment or not. Remember no limits. You can always revise.

The list will be as follows:

- Personal community
- Dream team
- Customer community

Step 2: Set dates on when you plan to reach out to your list and decide how to share your vision and goals on what it would mean to you to have them part of your community. For your customer community, this will take research, strategy, and planning to launch your customer community. Be sure to stick to your dates as you hit all of these points.

Step 3: Follow Up with your communities regularly

Get my interactive "Build a Community Checklist and Guide" to see what touch points you can add to your community today to enhance it at https://giftfrommelinda.com/.

The community saved my life, and it is why I have a business. Community is why I am unbreakable, unshakable, and unstoppable.

Have you built or refined your community to a strong and powerful community yet in your life? If not, what is stopping you?

 Born and raised in Brooklyn, NY, **Melinda Holmes**, certified wellness consultant at Above the Lead, had an entrepreneurial heart since Middle School. Her professional and entrepreneurial journey had many starts, stops, twists, and turns. For over 20 years, she worked in customer service in the insurance and tech industries while launching various side businesses, ranging from cake decorating and catering to holistic counseling. Melinda experienced a turning point due to losses and health challenges that made radical changes to her personal and professional life. Now she is more focused and action-driven than ever while being more patient and self-loving than before. As an Customer Experience Consultant, she combines her expertise in customer service with her training in holistic coaching to help small business owners rise above the rest in outstanding customer service and engagement. A process Melinda says is useful not only in business but also as a way of life. To learn more visit, https://www.abovethelead.com.

To connect contact me at: melindaholmes@abovethelead.com

To learn how a Community can increase your profits in your business please schedule 15 minutes to speak with me at ChatwithMelinda.com

CHAPTER 16

HEAR, HERE

PRESENT MOMENT LISTENING FOR LIFE-CHANGING RESULTS

Heather Jones, REALTOR®, ABR®

MY STORY

Work in Progress is the sign I focus on along my pathway towards self-improvement. It's a good reminder as there are ups and downs when learning to be different than before. Lately, I've started noticing my selective hearing. Sometimes listening, and sometimes not. The problem with this is when I ignore myself—that inner voice of truth—that is when I regret it. It won't take long before I get my feedback of defeat in a meltdown of tears. My divine inner guidance whispered ever so softly, *are you sure about this?* But I wasn't listening. I've forged ahead on another impossible plan to do way too many things in not enough time. Drats!

As I focus on self-awareness and become a better self-listener, I see it takes special attention to tune in to the interpersonal dialog within my being. My mind is so noisy and busy. It's a real struggle to hear anything else going on. I assess what has been working so far. I listen best with a quiet mind where I hear my stomach tell me how it feels. When I freely play in my imagination, I can hear my inner voice uninhibited by convention. When my heart beats, passionate and intense sounding my truth. I can hear it. This is when I find the clarity connecting me to the divine guidance that inspires me. Suddenly, infinite possibilities come together by magic, creating the most amazing experiences—significant transformation ripples through my soul as I discover what it means to listen in the present moment.

My feet ached after the long shift at the restaurant; my hair looked frazzled from the day, and my stomach kept growling. I imagined sitting down to a delicious dinner my boyfriend made for me during my drive home. "I thought you made dinner?" I asked as I came through the door, looking longingly at the empty dinner table. "Oh, I did. It's in the oven," he answered, briefly glancing up from the movie he was watching. I wasted no time discovering the decadent meal he had waiting for me. I hurried over to the oven, pulled the door open to see what was inside, and got a funny feeling as I suspiciously unwrapped the foil from the pan. Warning bells were going off in my head. I was highly concerned at that point. My nose scrunched up, afraid of the smell and what looked like greasy leather shoe soles. My brain was boiling. Did he expect me to eat this? It's not even edible! Who makes this for someone they "supposedly" love? In an instant, I knew it was over. Liver and onion tacos were my final straw.

It was good that this had happened now, I told myself. I want a man who can cook anyways. After several bad relationships, this break was long overdue. I needed time to figure myself out. The taco fiasco showed me I deserved more. Sitting at my kitchen table in my daydream—a handsome man is cooking for me. He is clean-shaven, dressed nicely with his sleeves rolled up. Lit candles flicker softly, illuminating the table where we're about to dine and fall in love. He opens a bottle of my favorite pinot noir. I smell the delicious smoky smell of the grill on his shirt as he pours the wine to let it breathe. He kneels in front of me, my heart flip-flopping in my chest. He takes off my boots, one at a time, and then rubs my tired feet. *Ding! Ah-ha!* A giant light bulb appears above my head. I desire a partner who tries to impress me! Someone else who shares my disdain for three-hour old liver and onion tacos on a Friday night. This fantasy man is someone I want to know. I must find him.

After my sexy epiphany, I began communicating with my higher power whenever possible, as much as possible. I prayed while pedaling across town or driving with my windows down. My hair whipped in the wind as I expressively asked for this ultimate person to appear. I would ask the universe, help me find the right man who would understand me, appreciate me, and love me unconditionally. I thought about him often, picturing him enjoying the activities I like most. We were profoundly in love, even before we met. I imagined how he looked at me, secure in who he was, solid and confident. He sees the love flickering in my eyes and knows I will always protect his heart.

My sister curled my hair, making sure I looked great for my 2 pm lunch date. I hop into my little retro Mercedes, and waving goodbye, she shouts, "Maybe he is the one!" I drive away smiling. I sneak into the bakery from the side door catching him off guard. Instantly, our eyes meet as a flash of electricity shocks me from head to toe. Our conversation flowed well from the beginning. We talked to each other, having a meaningful discussion of all the characters from *Winnie the Pooh*. He is just like Rabbit, who loves to garden and is always worried. I am Tigger, who looks for fun, not a care in the world. I could tell by his laugh at my date suggestion for liver and onion tacos that we were going to get along just fine. As we chatted, getting acquainted and enjoying our sandwiches, he reached over to me to brush carrot from my face. I leave our lunch date on cloud nine, feeling like I had met "the one."

The profound recognition of my needs changed my life incredibly. I found a way to provide the love I wanted by imagining my life with this person on my terms. I listened deeper into my soul, hearing the longing for a specific fitting partner who complimented my life in all regards. I established boundaries, declared my standard of care, and articulated my request for this person. Heather, your life will change only when you change. I heard the message ringing through me. I knew it was the absolute truth. The blessing of listening felt incredible as I transformed, creating my own story of happiness and unconditional love. I acknowledged my deepest desire for true honest love and partnership in this life. I discovered that I deserved my soul mate's highest caliber of love. I believed this so intensely I dreamed my fantasy man straight into my life. In a moment, I learned to be true to myself, be honest with my own needs, and listen to my innermost desires. I've never looked back since that lucky taco night. My life has grown immeasurably with love and happiness since finding the man of my dreams. He is every bit as wonderful and attentive as I imagined him that day in my kitchen.

"Just because you have the right to say something doesn't mean you should say it." A man exclaims to his group of friends in the line behind me. His words catch my attention as I stand there waiting to pick up my luggage. The simple clearness and assertiveness of his statement stood out. Was he telling his friends directly that he didn't want to listen to their opinion? It sure sounded like it. I move ahead in line, gathering my belongings. Then I jump on the shuttle zooming towards my hotel downtown. I continue to think about his assertion. I should have asked him why he said it. *Was he pointing out the opportunity that his friends had to interject, but he recommended they didn't?*

Later that evening, I sat alone in the hotel lounge. The table was small and round, with comfy pillows against the banquet. A cozy space to relax after the day's travels, it's warm and charming with historical elegance. I enjoy a glass of white wine, getting lost in my thoughts. I notice the people in front of me talking to each other at the bar. It's funny how much time we spend talking, almost constantly, unless we are alone. Eavesdropping is excellent entertainment for situations like this. I tune into the conversations floating in the air.

"I couldn't believe it when my date showed up late, and he looked like shit. I could tell he had an attitude right away," this lady exclaims to her friend next to her. I chuckle, doubting their compatibility as she describes his lackadaisical outfit compared to her seemingly fastidious demeanor. Just as I'm about to hear what happens next, her friend jumps in and begins a dating story of her own. *Wait, why didn't her friend ask more questions about the date?* I questioned silently, resisting the urge to interrupt the conversation. I imagine that this friend changed the focus of attention on purpose to be about her now. As she interjects a relatable story, a guise as her experience in the commonality of dating woes, I felt like shouting across the space, "Just because you have the right to say something doesn't mean you have to!" I doubt it would help or make any sense to a self-focused person. It didn't seem like the lousy date story was over yet. It was just getting started before the friend took over the conversation. The friends never make it back to the original crappy date story. I imagine a comical finale that seals the deal as the worst date in history. I just wanted to know more.

A friend of mine always says, "Read the room!" I love this statement because it reminds us to consider a greater awareness of others. It's essential to look at how we give attention and require others' attention when communicating. It's easy for the focus to change from one person to the next, almost without notice. What if your friend needed to share something important with you? Do you dominate the conversation to topics that interest you? Are you able to notice if others can fit into the conversation while you continually rattle on about yourself? I believe everyone has something to contribute. It's a response-ability as we communicate to share the floor and listen.

It takes only moments for someone to feel heard when you allow them to share their happiness or fears. In this time of uncertainty in the world, we must find conversations where we can hold open space so others can share what's in their hearts and minds. By doing this, we get to do an essential job of listening. People like to feel included and cherished. Listening is a privilege. They will appreciate you for sharing your space and being supportive of them. By the simple act of listening, you get to hear the needs of others. In this crucial role, you make a difference just by being present. How we show up for others is up to us. Can you ask for details about their day? If you do, they will see how much you care about them.

A flame shivers alone, its soul barely hanging on in the shadows of repression. The surrounding darkness reflects haunting eyes that stare straight at your vulnerability and weakness. Where can you hide? How can you escape the lows of loneliness and the disconnection of depression? Is it possible to emerge from the abyss of anguish alone? Can you survive the stormy seas of sadness to reach for the silver lining outside of grief? Who is the enemy to call out to fight when you're angry and filled with rage from the insufferable powerlessness we endure just trying to survive? Sick from biting our tongues, it hurts to speak.

We must look deeper and listen more closely. It is not easy to see suffering hiding behind someone's eyes. I reflect on the times when I've felt the sadness caused by depression and anguish. It was so lonely. I needed my family and friends. Identifying with others is extremely important, so you do not feel like you are the only one going through the dark times. There are caring people all around you and all over the world. Find your people who listen. Reaching out to others might not be easy, I believe in your power to respond appropriately to your own needs and take action. It may just be you imagining the conversation where you share what you're going through or what you need with a new friend. That is the start, the beginning of our change. Healing comes when we share our pain and fear. It will get better. No one needs to feel isolated or alone ever. Listen to your needs and act on them. This is how you can start being your own friend.

THE TOOL

Communication—Journal Exercises for Listening Awareness

#1 Listen to yourself.

How do you connect to your inner voice of truth? Are there times when it sounds louder and more evident? What is my intuition saying about my life right now? Am I choosing to listen or to ignore it?

#2 Observe your style.

Am I dominating the conversation or talking over others? Do I share too much or too little? Do I listen to what others say? Do I have questions that will draw others out to get to know them better?

Pay attention to your conversations throughout the day. It may be easiest to record them. Replay them as you write your observations in your journal. What are the main influences that affect the quality of dialog? Is someone pushing the conversation forward, keeping more on the surface rather than diving deeper into more intimate or emotional topics?

#3 Get the details.

Listen for the answers to these six questions.

1. **Who** is the main person or people involved?
2. **What** is the significant issue or problem that needs solving?
3. **When** does it need to be done?
4. **Why** is this important to the speaker?
5. **Where** can I get involved or find others to help?
6. **How** does the information pertain to the bigger picture?

Asking questions at an appropriate time without interrupting can also be helpful and show you are listening. What questions help you find out more details?

#4 Ways to grow.

If there were one thing you could change in communications, what would it be? Why? Would practicing a different style help you feel more confident?

I imagine I am speaking to a large crowd of people. I feel good, and the audience looks engaged. I don't often speak publicly, but visualizing that I am capable is one step closer to doing it.

#5 Engage in listening.

Listen as other people talk. What are some of the thoughts in your mind? Where is your focus? Did the speaker leave out any important details? How can I be more active or excited while in the listening role?

Keys to Present Moment Listening for Life-Changing Results

- Listen like your life depends on it; it does.
- Your life will change only when you change.
- Listen to yourself and do what is right for you.
- Listening is a privilege. Share your time and attention with others.
- Make connections daily with the people right in front of you.
- Know what is significant to yourself and others. Be significant.

Heather Jones has a never-give-up attitude. Her tenacity makes her *unstoppable* in her profession as a REALTOR® in Seattle. Customer service is her forte and getting to work directly with her clients is one of the best aspects of her career. She enjoys listening as clients share their stories, clarifying their needs and desires, and creating a customized strategy for the mission. Listening is vital to accomplishing all her objectives. Heather is your advocate, expert, and support to work with efficiently and trust.

In her personal life, being *unstoppable* means finding ways to help others. She wholeheartedly believes that we can come together to overcome any obstacle and end suffering for others. Heather is motivated by the generous nature of her friend and mentor, Alice Lamunu, who has made sponsoring education for girls in rural Northern Uganda possible through her non-profit organization Voices of Children's Faith in Northern Uganda. Due to the extreme poverty and lack of social service, its mission is to help girls through sponsorship have opportunities for education and vocational training they would not receive otherwise. Heather believes that her support and participation with VOCFINU is making a real difference in the lives of people who need help the most.

Catch up to Heather at https://www.seattlejones.com and

https://instagram.com/seattle.jones/

To learn more about how you can sponsor girls' education in Northern Uganda, please visit https://www.vocfinu.org

CHAPTER 17

SELF-WORTH

RECLAIM YOUR VOICE OF POWER AND BUILD THE LIFE OF YOUR DREAMS

Kimle Nailer, BA

"I was black before black was beautiful.
So compliments given to me were not that plentiful.
As a young girl, it didn't take long for me to realize
that I was not deemed beautiful in other people's eyes.
The shame I carried for being so black
wore on my young shoulders like a heavy sack.
My words were few, and I had few friends
all because I was not born with lighter skin."

~Kimle Nailer

MY STORY

Tears and sadness were common experiences of my childhood. The pain I felt inside held me hostage, from simply enjoying the simple things most little girls my age found enjoyable. Bullying was a regular childhood experience at school from first grade until I entered the sixth grade at a small christian church in Canton, Ohio. In addition, being the eighth of ten children, I easily got lost in the shuffle of everyday life. I also have five sisters, all prettier than me, which I assumed because they received compliments I never heard. I was born a little black girl with dark skin in 1963, long before the *My Black is Beautiful* campaign came along. The shame I felt based on my skin tone led me on a path of low self-esteem and plenty of hardships, constantly looking for validation, affection, and love. It would take many years to rediscover myself, find purpose, and create the life of my dreams.

I couldn't wait to begin school. There were no pre-schools when I was a little girl, so I was five years old when I started school. I remember seeing my brothers and sisters leave for school, and I couldn't wait to go. Kindergarten was my happy place. I loved my kindergarten teacher, Ms. O'Cheski, who let me help out in the classroom. I was a teacher's pet, and I loved all the attention and soaked it up like a dry sponge. "What else can I do," I would ask to keep her attention. From this experience, I realized if you help others, they will love you. I decided to do everything in my power to earn love and spent the next three decades doing so.

This excitement from going to school was short-lived. I will never forget a boy from my first-grade classroom asking, "Why are you so black?" Laughter broke out in the room. I had no answer and stood there staring at him. The top of my ears began to burn with anger. I was hurt deeply by his words, but I didn't want him to see me cry. I stomped away, saying, "You are so silly." The chair legs screeched on the floor as I flopped down in my chair, crossed my arms, and dropped my head. My classmates continued to laugh until the teacher stopped them. I sat there thinking, *why do I have to be so different from everyone else? If my skin was lighter I could have friends too.* The pain of their laughter pierced my soul. Little did I know from that experience I would start a behavior pattern that would follow me into my mid-30s of hiding away and sitting on the sideline.

I was no happier at home because my siblings also teased me. I was regularly referred to as the darkest girl in the family. School was my escape. *Why am I the darkest girl? How did my skin get so dark?* I asked myself. I felt like an outcast, and being in the sibling lineup between two sisters who were much lighter than me didn't help. I constantly heard how cute they were because they were light-skinned. Never did anyone call me cute. Isolation began early for me because of my dark skin. I felt as if I didn't matter at all.

I never felt special until my grandmother gave me a pet name, Little Monkey. She started calling me her little monkey, and I loved this special attention, but it infuriated my mom. "Mother, didn't I tell you to stop calling her that? Don't call her that, and I mean it." They would get into an argument over and over. My grandmother would say, "Baby, I don't mean no harm. That's just my cute little name for you," as she embraced me. My mother didn't understand that I didn't care about those words; I enjoyed the attention, which felt good.

Later my mom sent me to a small christian school in North Canton, Ohio, when I entered the sixth grade. In July, I turned 11 years old and was excited to go because I wouldn't be teased like at my old school. Although there was no more teasing, I was sent to Ohio to go to school without my mom. I was not prepared for that experience at all.

My two sisters, three cousins, and another friend from our church in Detroit, Michigan, left home to attend this Ohio school. The seven of us were the only black kids from kindergarten to twelfth grade in the entire school. The culture shock was overwhelming, and we lived with families we'd never seen. They were clueless about black people, but we were all part of this christian community my mom joined. This experience would last the next seven years of my life, further eroding any confidence, value, or self-worth I had. My acceptance of being black became a greater challenge in an all-white world, ignorant of my culture, and challenging my blackness.

Once my sisters and I were expelled from school because we were "black militants" wearing afros. During the 1970s, the "I'm Black, and I'm Proud" movement was symbolized by wearing afros in support of that message. However, for my sisters and me, we were not wearing afros for any movement. Nestled in an Amish country with no media outlets to the outside world, we didn't know any such movement existed.

Enrolling in a swimming class was part of the school's requirement. What these white people didn't know was that when black hair gets wet, the pressed-straight locks return to their natural curls—the look of an afro. Imagine what a little girl already trapped in dark skin feels, and now she has to feel ashamed of her hair? Some relief came when the school called my mother to tell her about my behavior. My mom explained the process of black hair getting pressed to be straight, but that the natural state is curly hair. We were then told we could not take swimming class, even though we had to go to the swim class and watch everyone else swim.

Imagine seven inner-city black kids from Detroit arriving in Ohio's Amish country to go to a small school. The christian love was real, but it didn't trump the lack of knowledge they had regarding black people. I lived there until I graduated from high school. This church denomination was not Amish, but there were many similar values. Seclusion from the outside world was a shared value. Living on farms away from the city to ensure the world did not influence us meant no TVs, radios, or any outside engagement with others not in the organization. This would be my school experience until I graduated in 1981.

At a time when Madonna and Michael Jackson were topping the charts, I was clueless about it all. This lifestyle created a tunnel vision of the world for me, and it became very difficult to trust and connect to people outside of the community. My farming lifestyle made it difficult to transition to city life after graduation. I felt lost and had no sense of purpose. To maintain the community, we had schedules and routines that kept us busy cooking, farming, doing laundry, taking care of children, etc. I never did anything but what was on the schedule. After years of structured living, I could not be an individual with my thoughts, desires, or wishes. The result was withdrawal. I felt inadequate to live in a world I had never experienced.

Imagine trying to transition into a woman, a black woman at that, with no point of reference. My lack of confidence eroded my self-esteem further. In addition, my home was now community living, much like the farms where other families shared rooms in our house. Individuality was not encouraged, although a necessary tool to build your dreams and a future. I developed no sense of self to grow confidently into womanhood. I had no idea of who I was or who I wanted to be. My life eventually became stifled, passionless, and hopeless.

My uncertainties impacted my relationship when a gentleman in the church community expressed interest in me. I didn't have any physical attraction to him but fell prey to my usual behavior—people-pleasing for affection. I tried to make myself have feelings, after all, I never had a boyfriend or compliments from any man. I relocated to Chicago, Illinois, to pursue this relationship, which quickly deteriorated and became abusive. Three years later, I returned to Detroit, depressed and over 25 thousand dollars in debt from him demanding money from my credit cards to fund his business. Months of therapy, medication, and counseling revealed my desperation for love and validation had prevented me from having healthy boundaries—a necessity for healthy relationships.

However, this experience changed my life and opened a whole new world to me, one in which I discovered I had a voice. I began to reconnect with myself, and I discovered my self-worth. I understood that having value was not only necessary to interact with the world but also impacted how I related to my peers, chose careers, selected a partner, built friendships, and cared for my body and health. I became present to live the life of my dreams.

It took years before I understood this valuable lesson of self-worth, but I no longer obsessed over validation from others. The heaviness, sadness, and depression were the result of people-pleasing. When I freed myself from looking to others, I found a new world within that propelled me forward. I found my inner essence of beauty that wasn't limited to skin tones.

My self-love created a burning desire to experience myself. A passion for exploring life on my terms guided me. The world was not out there but originated from within with no need for outside validation. A renewed sense of self filled me with passion. A passion that birthed a purpose for my life to light the way for other women and girls struggling with low self-esteem. I became the founder of Positive S.I.S.T.E.R.S. (*Self-Improvement Simply Takes Education, Redevelopment, and Sincerity*), a movement to empower women to know their value and to know their worth. I hosted workshops and trained to become a coach. Speaking opportunities and book projects allowed me to be a blessing to others. New opportunities continuously exploded in my life from understanding and living my purpose.

It's often said that how we start has nothing to do with where we end up.

My life is a testament to that truth. It took a depression to awaken me, but that experience not only opened my eyes but opened my heart to understand all the decisions I made along my life's journey. As I embraced the pain of my childhood, I reflected on my decisions and determined my pain would not govern me.

Instead, those memories birthed my life's purpose to help other women choose to become unstoppable. I found new confidence from within that gave me new guidance and freedom to map a new direction for my life. I now sat in the driver's seat, knowing I was not bound to the opinion or approvals of others. I unleashed my soul's essence to guide me. Today, I am living the life of my dreams, unencumbered by the outside influence of others' opinions.

I discovered pain comes from looking outward and then assessing yourself in comparison to a set of surroundings or values from others. It's taking inventory of other people's ideas and frameworks to see if you measure up. This external evaluation will keep you feeling sad, depressed, or overwhelmed. Until my mid-30s, that's how I lived, just going through the motions of life with no drive or ambition. Today my life is full of purpose, and I want you to know that you can also step into the S.P.O.T.L.I.G.H.T. (*Shift Position of Thinking and Live In God's Highest Truth*) of your life and shine as a gift for others. Embracing your pain in love will shift your identity so you can live in God's highest truth about you.

My desire is no longer just to work but live a purpose-filled life. I elevated my career by obtaining a degree and creating career opportunities with multiple promotions quickly. I have become an entrepreneur, coaching women and girls and hosting annual events encouraging women to come together to heal and unleash their voice of power.

I expanded my real estate business, became a licensed builder, and launched Nail-Rite Construction Company. I consistently attracted the support I needed to grow as I aligned my soul's essence.

Imagine a little black girl, once filled with pain and sadness, who goes from living in Amish country of Ohio to building an arena for a National Hockey League in Detroit, Michigan. Great things await you also on the other side of all your life's pain. Renew your self-worth because you, too, are unstoppable!

THE TOOL

The lessons shared from my journey are to give you hope so you can also move past your pain, find a purpose for your life, and rediscover your voice of power. Becoming unstoppable is the result of having a deep connection to your heart, which empowers you to see your true self-worth and value. This transformation from pain to passion occurs when you embrace your inner essence.

I would like to share the process I used that allowed me to know I was bigger than my pain, bigger than my life's experiences, and an unstoppable force. This exercise has two phases, Deconstruction and Reconstruction, to help you transform your self-worth and value. During the deconstruction phase, play soft, relaxing music and speak these words (or the words of your choice) to yourself:

I am Worthy. I deserve love. I deserve joy. I am protected. I am guided by God. I am Loved. I am worthy of every desire of my heart. I am Divine. I am one with God. I am one with the Universe. I am anchored in love. My being is filled with light.

After speaking these words, allow yourself to bask in the music. Repeat the statements, each time breathing deeply, allowing your stomach to rise on the inhale and fall on each exhale. Now imagine your body being deconstructed into small atomic particles. Imagine your skin and hair dissolving into tons of tiny atoms and disappearing. Breathing deeply, imagine every other system of your body dissolving: your muscles, nerves, bones, and organs dissipating into thin air. As you exhale, see the molecular particles expanding. Now be aware of your presence and consciousness without your body. Feel your power. Feel your true essence. Your body does not define you! Speak those words to yourself again and bask in this powerful space of knowing your true self.

Now begin the reconstruction. Conscious of yourself without form, breathe your body back together. Command your organs to return to your body, your nervous system, your circulatory system, your skeletal system, your muscular system, and see your skin encompass it all together. Breathe in deeply as each system is reconstructed.

Upon completion of this exercise, fill your heart with love. Remember a powerful, loving experience and just feel it in your heart. Now embrace every painful experience, reframing it from your place of power. Imagine each situation being absorbed in love in your heart. See yourself as a little girl and shower her with all the love she never felt. This little one is you, the newly reconstructed you filled with love and power!

This is the opening step of my program, *Transform your Self-worth into Net Worth*. Without releasing your pain, you can't open your heart to feel safe or valued. A closed heart prevents discovering your purpose and passion, causing you to feel powerless. When I felt this love in my own heart, I no longer struggled with looking at others' physical bodies to find my worth. Instead, I embraced me, loved me, and savored the peace I found inside me, which made me unstoppable. I was now the source of the love I desired. You can experience this tool (coming soon) at www.positivesisters.com/restore.

Holding onto pain only keeps you stuck in shame and blame, creating low self-esteem. I no longer needed external validation to find my worth when I looked inside my heart. Instead, I embraced me, loved me, and I savored the peace I found within. My new purpose emerged to help other girls and women find their inner essence of beauty and connect to their soul's purpose. I was home in my heart to share this love with others like never before. No delivery service will leave a valuable package at your home without someone being present to sign and accept the package. Your heart is no different. You must be present to know yourself. Reconnect with your heart and release yourself from all the beliefs you held about yourself that are not true so your purpose can emerge.

As I welcomed the lessons from each experience, I accepted my decisions and now make better choices that support me. My past no longer defines or confines me to living with low self-esteem. My black skin uncovered my inner essence of beauty that exceeds any physical attribute of my body.

Kimle Nailer is a successful, heart-centered entrepreneur who uses her life's story of overcoming low self-esteem due to her skin's dark color as a compelling message to teach women how to transform self-worth into net worth to become a confident businesswomen.

Ms. Nailer holds a business degree from Wayne State University. Before transitioning into Construction, she successfully built her career working at major firms, including J. D. Powers and Associates, Ford Motor Company, and GTB, formerly Team Detroit.

She also is a real estate investor, fixing and flipping properties for financial stability and passive income. Her real estate business provides financial freedom to travel and pursue her passion of teaching women to transform self-worth into net-worth for career advancement. She empowers women to become confident businesswomen and serial entrepreneurs.

Ms. Nailer became a licensed builder and launched Nail-Rite Construction Company which provides residential and commercial services. Her construction background led to co-authoring Wealth for Women: Conversations with the Team that Creates the Dream and connected her to the Real Estate Investor Goddess Community.

Ms. Nailer is an active member of the National Association of Black Women in Construction (NABWIC), where she serves as the National President. She recently became a board member for Michigan Women's Forward, a non-profit that provides funding for female entrepreneurs, and was appointed to the City of Eastpointe Planning Commission.

To receive support to transform pain to passion and self-worth to net worth, visit www.positivesisters.com to schedule your complimentary session.

Follow us at:

www.twitter.com/positivesisters

www.facebook.com/mypositivesisters

CHAPTER 18

A SIMPLE TOOL
TO TRUST YOURSELF AGAIN

STRENGTHEN THE BELIEF IN YOURSELF
SO YOU BECOME UNSTOPPABLE

Nicole Batiste, Attuned Inner Life Coach

MY STORY

I was an addict with several addictions. I hid it in plain sight for a long time. It wasn't until I was over one hundred thousand dollars in credit card debt that friends and family urged me to stop.

Drug users, retail therapy, sugar addiction all have a foundation of masking a feeling. My addictions were a cycle of buying personal and business development programs, not finishing them, and buying some more. I experienced the classic addiction signs of hope and let down every time I signed up for a new program. I may have even been addicted to the disappointment.

I don't know why I keep buying these courses; I never finish them. Days turned into weeks, months, and years and those courses remained undone. Neglecting to follow through these courses reinforced an underlying belief that I am a failure. The reinforced belief deepened my lack of self-trust. Over the years, the resultant debt and unfinished programs weighed on me like a ton of bricks. There was so much guilt and shame. I never realized how much energy the unfinished projects consumed.

The lack of self-trust didn't start with my addiction, though. Early childhood trauma opened that door. Time and again, I neglected to hold up my end of the bargain with myself. I kept trying to commit, but I continued to fall short. The earliest I can recall this pattern of behavior was when I handed in my dog-shaped book report when I was in the third grade.

We were all in our seats in class. The normal chatter came to a halt at the sound of Ms. Smith's soft yet assertive voice. "Okay, everyone, hand in your book reports." She was sitting at her desk in front of the class with her hand open in an expectant gesture of receipt. She smiled at each student as they handed in their reports. I walked to the front of the classroom, smiled, and handed her a dog-shaped report before returning to my seat. The smile was my mask, though. And my report was a representation of how I felt deep down. On the outside, creative and interesting. Yet on the inside, incomplete, unworthy, and "just enough" to get by.

Any time I attempted something new, it was always half-hearted, despite thinking otherwise. Don't get me wrong, I work hard, but I was missing a key component, and that was being committed 100%. The results proved it, but I did not feel the need to do better. I received compliments for the work I did on a regular basis, so I did nothing to improve it, not realizing the internal damage it was doing to my psyche.

I never finish anything! As an adult, the lack of self-trust perpetuated a cycle of inability to show up anywhere 100%. Wherever I was, I was already somewhere else. "Sorry I'm late" became so common. The "sorry" was akin to crying wolf. Friends and family gave me an earlier "report" time to increase the odds I'd show up on time.

One evening, I was sitting on my living room floor decluttering and going through old papers. I paused for a moment and looked around, thinking about all the stuff I had accumulated over the years. I became filled with sadness and frustration as I thought about how the things that bring me joy went untouched for years. My piano was out of tune; my viola was collecting dust; my arts and craft projects remained incomplete. The tears started rolling down my face. *What's wrong with me that I can't stick to any one thing?* At that time, I didn't know to correlate my childhood patterns to my behavior. I didn't realize that asking, "What's wrong with me?" didn't help me address the deeper issue. And I had no clue that childhood trauma also played a role.

Psychology Today listed traits of someone who is self-trusting in a blog post. Here's an exert of that post:

". . .they have clarity and confidence in their choices. They are interdependent, which includes healthy dependency, not overly dependent or hyper-independent. They speak with authority that comes from a deep place within but is not arrogant. They are good observers and have cultivated the ability to learn from their experiences, both the successes and failures. Because they can trust themselves to not be punitive when they make mistakes, they can look openly at their experience without fear of self-punishment."

Self-punishment. When I finally looked back on that time, it was like I was punishing myself for not finishing things by signing up for more programs that kept me in debt and too busy to do the things I enjoyed. An attempt to get a handle on my debt caused me to get a second job. My hours increased, yet my habits didn't change. That deepened my lack of self-trust as I began to question my judgment.

As you can imagine, not being able to trust your own judgment doesn't help you achieve greatness. In my mind, though, if I don't go all in, I won't be as hurt if something doesn't pan out. *If I give it my all and I still don't make it, that means I'm not good enough.* I believed this statement for years but didn't know it! It didn't matter that those words were not expressed. My actions continued to show that subconscious belief founded on distrust. Remember the dog-shaped book report? I summarized the summary. I never read the book. I put all my effort into the outer appearance in hopes that it looked like I put in the work. I received an 'A,' which, in my mind, confirmed I didn't have to give it my all, and I'd be fine. As such, that pattern continued into adulthood, as noted previously. I have since learned that there is a greater sense of fulfillment in "failing" from trying your best than there is in not trying as hard. I've learned that it doesn't mean you're not good enough; in fact, I would challenge you to try to prove that thought right. I will show you what I mean later.

Something's got to give. I always struggled with losing stuff in my house, showing up late, not showing up at all, forgetting things. *I am so tired of feeling overwhelmed all the freaking time! Why am I always behind on everything?* For the record, those questions are not necessarily productive, but it at least shows there is an awareness that something had to change. I finally acknowledged that what I was doing wasn't working because I wanted to be better. I learned how to ask better questions. I learned how to identify the underlying cause directing my actions. I'm still tackling tardiness in some areas of my life (ask the editor and publisher). The difference between today and the past is this isn't a result of a lack of trust. Alright, I digress. A very helpful question on my quest was: *How can I start learning to trust myself?*

That was the start of the shift to becoming unstoppable. In fact, that was where Google and I started my quest to address my self-trust issues. I was already an avid reader of personal development books. It's where I found many of my mentors who helped me level up in other areas of my life. So I knew the next step to leveling up meant doing some work. I started searching for books to help me improve my habits. I was also exposed to the concept of the power of my words and how they can improve my inner relationship or keep it in turmoil. It's a choice.

I started becoming more mindful of how I described myself and my actions. I learned how my subconscious ensures I achieve what I believe, not what I say. Its fertile soil will grow whatever I plant. So I started planting intention and empowerment. I started giving myself grace and being kind as I learned new habits.

When your words say "yes," but your subconscious says "no," your results will mirror your beliefs. In so doing, you reinforce the limiting beliefs. I started building my self-efficacy toolbox to strengthen the bond and trust relationship with myself. And I get so much joy from sharing the tools with clients.

One of my favorite and quite effective tools I've come up with is the *Prove It or Lose & Replace It Method.* Gaining the ability to recall personal wins and recognize strengths makes this method effective. It's especially helpful at preventing you from talking yourself out of an opportunity due to fear and lack of self-trust.

THE TOOL

THE TOOL: PROVE IT OR LOSE & REPLACE IT METHOD

Imagine if someone accused you of being mean. You'd say, "Prove it!" Yet when we call ourselves names like that, we don't stop to ask for proof. And years of planting those rotten seeds into your subconscious mind's fertile soil produces rotten outcomes. Okay, maybe not rotten, but they certainly don't produce the fruit we want. Being able to recognize the thoughts that talk you out of an opportunity gives you the chance to challenge them. It gives you a moment to say, "Prove it!" to yourself. As such, you're able to make a decision from an empowered state. When you're unaware of them, you continue to believe your beliefs and wonder why things aren't going as intended. I want to help you develop a listening ear so you can catch and counter the non-supportive thoughts. Practicing thought awareness on a consistent basis is an exercise that strengthens many muscles, including your self-trust muscle.

What does it mean to "Prove, Lose, and Replace?" Great question!

'Prove It' encourages you to acknowledge the limiting beliefs preventing you from moving forward. Once acknowledged, you challenge that belief by searching for evidence in your past that the thought or belief is right. If you discover that there's nothing in your past performance that can prove that thought right, then 'Lose & Replace' that thought. If you do find something in your past to prove that thought right, there is other inner work that needs to take place first. For that, I invite you to check out The N.I.K.K.I. Method included in the resource document.

For now, let's break *Prove It or Lose & Replace It* down further into steps.

Step 1: Acknowledge the limiting belief thoughts talking you out of what you want to do. Let's use dance as an example. Limiting beliefs, excuses, or reasons that would prevent you from dancing could be:

I can't dance.

I look silly.

I'm too old.

I may hurt myself.

I don't know what I'm doing.

Step 2: Prove those thoughts to be true by asking questions such as: Says who? By who's standard? Who made that rule? In truth, more often than not, you won't need to go too deep here because you already know that thought is false. If you don't prove that thought to be true, move to step three.

Step 3: Lose & Replace It. If there is no evidence that proves that thought true, why hold on to it? Be intentional about removing it from your mindset and replacing it with the truth. For example:

I can't dance. Says who? Prove it! You don't find any proof, so lose it. Let that thought go forever and replace it with what's going on. When you release that limiting thought, you give yourself a chance to be heard. And you find out that it's not that you don't think you can't dance, it's that you're not comfortable dancing in public.

The **Lose & Replace** part of the method empowers you to take ownership of the real reason you're hesitating. If it ends up that you're scared, so what? That's quite normal. What does matter is understanding where your responses come from so you can make well-informed decisions.

Listen to Kris and Sam as they show what it looks like in "real-time" and see if you can tell when Sam is using the *Prove It or Lose & Replace It Method.*

Scenario 1:

Kris: "Hey Sam, I'm creating a project and thought about you. Your ability to motivate and inspire people will be so helpful. Are you in?"

Sam: "Wow! Thanks, but *(I don't know how to do that, what if I fail, I'll say I'm busy)* I'm not sure I'll have the time to support."

Kris: "Oh, okay. Well thanks anyway."

Scenario 2:

Kris: "Hey Sam, I'm creating a project and thought about you. Your ability to motivate and inspire people will be so helpful. Are you in?"

Sam: "Wow! Thanks *(I don't know how to do that, what if I fail? but I've done things like this in the past, this could be a great opportunity)* I would love to join you!"

Kris: "Yay! Thank you so much!"

If you guessed Sam is using the method in scenario two, you're right. You can see how subtle the shift is, right? The truth is, not knowing what to do in a different situation doesn't mean you don't know what to do at all. It means you haven't done it in that capacity. In that case, you pull your current knowledge into the new venture. You gain even more knowledge going through the process, which sharpens the tool (a.k.a you), making you even more valuable. Fully showing up even through fear builds self-trust. Proving unsupportive thoughts wrong builds self-trust. Reminding yourself where you've succeeded before is golden. The only things that make the new situation different are your thoughts about it and the situation itself.

Side Note: If you have a hard time recalling when you did something well, I want to encourage you to keep a small notebook with you and write down moments you secretly feel proud of. Build up your vault of supportive evidence of your greatness. And get comfortable acknowledging where you shine.

The beautiful thing about this tool is it removes you from the tendency to judge yourself or beat yourself up for having unsupportive thoughts. It empowers you by encouraging you to create a practice of recalling your knowledge and strengths.

Have you noticed the common thread throughout this chapter? You. **You are** the tool. All of the knowledge you have cannot be taken from you. You can only obtain more. The key is having a deep sense of knowing that you've got this. That comes from reminding yourself of what you do know rather than focusing on what you don't. That comes from asking the right questions when you realize you're feeling stuck or the same outcomes continue to present themselves. It comes from understanding that your knowledge and skillset go wherever you go. That's your value. No matter what the circumstance is, understanding your value is what makes you unstoppable.

If this tool doesn't resonate with you (or even if it does), I invite you to explore some of the other tools I've come up with to keep my clients and me moving forward. Scan this QR code to access the resource document. This document will change as more tools and techniques are proven, so check back from time to time.

Finally, embody the feeling of knowing that you are indeed unstoppable. Can you feel it? What does it feel like to hold your head high and be admired as much as you admire others who made the decision to show up and be unstoppable? Sit in that for a bit and imagine what that feels like with as many of your senses as you can. Create a picture or whole story in your mind that supports the person you're becoming.

Now, decide today to be who you just envisioned because you have everything you need to excel no matter where you are right now or where you started. You are one decision away from being unstoppable. Now go and be your great self!

Nicole Batiste is an Attuned Inner Life Coach and speaker. She is a certified holistic and functional medicine health coach with a drive to learn how the mind can support you and your goals. That drive gives her the passion for helping women see how amazing they are, which allows them to step into their powerful selves. Her gift of getting some of the most closed women to open up about their challenges has created shifts and growth in many lives.

She founded Be Well with N.I.K.K.I. to support those who know what it means to feel like they live two lives that are not in alignment. One inside their mind and one that everyone else sees. She helps her clients bridge the gap between where they are and where they want to be using her created methods. Realizing the foundation of "stuckness" in the "real" world is the "stuckness" we hold onto in our mind— most of the time without knowing it. Nicole created several methods to help clients push past those holds, and she teaches them how to support themselves through their challenges. Self-acceptance, self-compassion, self-trust, self-love, and self-care are common results. To learn more, visit www.bewellwithnikki.com.

CHAPTER 19

BLUE CHAKRA

HOW TO INCREASE SELF-CONFIDENCE
AND HAVE WHIP APPEAL IN YOUR LIFE AND BUSINESS

Dr. Nailah G. Beraki-Pierre, Ph.D.

I dedicate this chapter to my queen mother,
Ina Lee Green; Fearless!

To be a business owner is one of the most rewarding and challenging things you can do. You can finally live your passion. As the boss, you are the business. You cannot be fired. You are responsible for everything. You're a speaker; your voice is everything! You think about everything you can to keep yourself healthy balanced, and whole, so why shouldn't your business be any different? I've noticed that sometimes our voices get suppressed. It affects every area of our life. We spend so much of our time at work or in our business that we begin to look at the energy—what blocks it, the pain it causes, and the courage to overcome it and become grounded.

We look around from every angle wondering why a particular formula does not work and mentally add a lot of possibilities. Life happens! Yet, when we think about our business, energy, and effectiveness, fear shows up and plays a significant part in every area of our lives.

MY STORY

Life was good. I worked hard and enjoyed the freedom of having my say in my business and my life. I loved being in a community living in sunny Southern California. It was fascinating, so different from New York. Then, one day, my life changed. I was struck by a vehicle that left me in a coma and paralyzed on my left side. My world stood still. My gift was always in service to helping people, and I was great at that and making money for the services rendered.

After the accident, I was not able to. I had to learn how to save myself, heal myself and make a living. I had to learn how to survive, including how to walk and regain my voice again. What happens to a dream deferred? How do you face your life when all hell is breaking loose? You need to know how to survive when things do not go the way you planned. To be able to stand in the rain, vulnerable and alone, and still have faith without knowing which way your life is going. Can I tell you how grateful I am to my parents for teaching us how to pray and trust in God? Was I put to the spiritual test during my new circumstances? I spent two months in the hospital and left in a wheelchair with the prognosis of doing crossword puzzles and, my voice did not seem to matter, only their prognosis. I knew God had another plan for my life, and it was more significant than I could imagine. After returning the wheelchair months later, the doctors asked me how I got well. I used my voice to release blue chakra energy and decided that I would not live their prognosis no matter what. As a result of that experience, I had uncovered new strengths within myself.

TOOLS FROM THIS EXPERIENCE

I want to share a few of the lessons I learned from the experience:

Begin to identify yourself. Not just your name, gender, age, and occupation, but who you are as a person, your likes and dislikes, and your strengths.

1. Discover something new about yourself every day. Do not take yourself for granted.

2. Become a more confident person. To increase your self-esteem, become grounded in the face of adversity as well as in joyful times.

ABOUT THAT BLUE CHAKRA

So, what is a chakra? The term chakra is a system of energy. The word chakra comes from Sanskrit, and it means wheel or disc; these wheels are like CDs or floppy disks that we used to use in our computers. And each chakra manages a different set of programs such as our relationships, language, and feelings programs stored in memories. Chakras exist at the meeting point of the mind and body, yet they have a location in the physical body.

Energy interacts between the unconscious mind and the physical body. Even though chakras are not physical like an organ or bone, the chakras do influence your experience of the physical body. For example, butterflies in your stomach, a frog in your throat, and aching in your back can influence the chakras. In those areas, the chakras are not spinning; they are stuck. They affect us in our personal and in our business life. I chose the blue chakra to share with you in this short chapter because, as speakers, healers, and entrepreneurs, this is the energy that, when blocked, invites fear. More information on the seven chakras can be found in the book *Wheels of Life* by author Anodea Judith. The blue chakra is responsible for communication, creativity, and self-expression. It's the communication center for your business, finding your authentic business voice connecting on stage and asking for money. The blue chakra represents the throat, associated with the color light blue or turquoise; it's all about expression and truth, so we can communicate our reality in our voice clearly and effectively, and guess what, fear wants your voice and your business.

My mom gave me a piece of advice when I was a teenager to never say in anger what you don't mean because you can say you're sorry, but you can't take it back. It takes a few words to hurt someone. Wounds heal, but they leave scars that never disappear. Words have power. The throat chakra has power. It can bring you joy or cause misery. Proverbs 18:21 puts it this way: "The tongue has the power of life and death. The stakes are high. Your words can speak life, or your words can talk about death, you can build others up, or you can tear them down." The Blue Chakra is powerful; we are powerful.

Everyone has experienced what it's like to have that feeling of being stuck or caught in your throat chakra, that certain "cat got your tongue" feeling when you can't seem to speak. We notice the way our voice gets small and tight and makes us appear nervous. All trapped energy, traumas, and disappointment reside in the throat. This blue chakra represents our ability to receive, assimilate, store, and express communication in the neck at the meeting point between the head and the body. The energy is palpable; you can see it and feel it immediately when it's there. That's because the throat chakra is one of the main stops, like a bottleneck.

I remember walking up to the stage; the closer I got to the microphone, the more my throat seemed to tighten up. I felt like I was going through a metamorphosis. My insides didn't feel that connection when I began to speak. It's a very vulnerable feeling. I didn't run; I made no excuses. I kept going, and as I continued to talk, my voice became more assertive and more straightforward; I felt connected from the inside out and could communicate with my audience.

I used a breathing technique to fully come into my body and listen and receive that internal recharge. That is the power of the blue chakra; you can transform yourself. It's powerful. So, what happens when communication is stuck? It impacts us. What happens when a child can't tell anyone what happened at school or can't tell their teacher they're abused at home? What happens when we tell a lie to survive?

Because our situation is so hard to believe, our behavior contradicts the experience of what's happening.

"Fear is not real. The only place that fear can exist is in our thoughts of the future. It's a product of our imagination, causing us to fear things that do not at present and may not ever exist. Do not misunderstand me; danger is very real, but fear is a choice."

~Will Smith

The purpose of the blue chakra, the fifth chakra, is to find harmony, fully living to speak our truth.

Fear can be draining. A client of mine, Dee, said she was fearful of failing; she was accomplishing her goals in the present time but reliving past mistakes that led her to question her every move—sometimes being paralyzed by it all, she restricted her voice. She sabotaged herself to keep from advancement.

Fear is so busy; it's easier to use your voice to tell someone you're stressed out than to say, "I'm afraid someone else is threatening to steal my job."

How does fear show up for you in the workplace and in relationships? The thread is always there. It's all about how we approach it, respond to it, learn from it, live it, and pivot away from it.

When does it show up for you? If you develop a relationship with fear and confront whatever you feel worried about, many times, you'll find it's self-inflicted. Now you're deciding to use good fear. The change of mind and commitment will win.

Fear usually doesn't bother you if you're not doing anything. It hangs out on the sidelines, waiting for you to become inspired, waiting for your genius to come and visit you with ideals and vision of what could be. However, faith without work is dead.

This fear creates the same sensations within you that good fear does. You still feel increased heart rate, extra blood flow to the extremities, and rapid, short breathing. This fear says you're not good enough. "I can't do this," "I can't make it," "I could have," "I would have, if…"

This bad fear may show up as a lack of confidence, low self-esteem, beliefs, or doubts that limit your activities and functionality in your day-to-day personal or business life. You've likely heard, or perhaps even said something like, "I'd love to be recognized as a great speaker, but I'm so scared of speaking in public." This irrational fear is keeping you from your most whole life. Unfortunately, some of us have an automatic setting on our fear that kicks in just before we can claim success. You may even limit your success due to the unwanted limelight.

When we get scared, we believe the situation is causing the fear. It's in your mind, but your mind will find a way to rationalize what it wants you to think. Listening to that voice that says, *you'll look foolish for getting up to speak*, is severely limiting your success.

When you're fearful, you cannot think straight. When you cannot believe, you cannot accomplish anything. This is how fear creates the feelings connected to our throat chakra and steals our voice.

Now meet fear's cousin, procrastination. He lives here too. Fear of the phone may cause you to create long lists of prospects because you will not pick up that phone. Instead, you may find yourself doing laundry, washing the car, or reorganizing your file cabinet. When we fear to do an activity, it's only natural to find a more enjoyable activity to fill the time. You do not feel guilty because you're doing something, but nothing. This fear is stopping your business dead. Procrastination will not gain you clients or cash flow.

Self-sabotage, fear's second cousin, also lives here. Sometimes we let our past fears prevent us from moving on with life. Fear can affect you in very subtle ways. A client, Jackie, continually criticizes her ex-husband. This ex-husband has remarried and has a new family. This divorce happened ten years ago. She continues reliving the past, preventing her from moving on and living a whole life. This energy is blocking her blue chakra and holding fear to prevent the release of the past. Negative thoughts of her failed relationship fill her mind constantly because she has so few people in her life.

It's challenging to unwrap all our fears and 'head junk' and keep it unwrapped. We tend to slip right back in because it feels comfortable. There are things you can do to put fear on the run.

It takes a journey, and if you stay on your path, you can heal your life by learning the lessons and blessings.

Emotional pain does not heal until we practice forgiveness. Consciously you may not be aware of these feelings of fear and where they came from until we bring them up and look at them. If you can sit down with your fear and bring it up to the conscious level, you can experience freedom. From negative fear, use this re-healthy fear as an ally. Peace and forgiveness are inner acts. An inward journey of letting go of the pain is one of the most influential works you will do in your life. When you decide to forgive, you release yourself from that person, thing, or memory—you know when you're sick and tired of being sick and tired within yourself. We learned to react to, not respond, from what we know is the truth. We decide, *this is not going to take me out.* You want to convince your subconscious, your mind. Your higher self already knows the truth. The emotional part—the feeling part of your nature—lets go. Then, we must repeat the statement enough so that the feeling part of you inherits this new way of being, and your body and mind change.

Let go. Releasing ourselves from anger helps release the fear. The pain is gone because you are at peace. I affirm. I remove and let go of this situation that no longer has power over me.

This intuition relates to pure consciousness itself. Good, healthy fear combined with wisdom is like a tightrope between two fixed anchors. And you're the tightrope walker. As you walk between them, you see where you want to go and what needs doing. You reach toward balance, patience. Mindful intention for now and good fear will gladly give us that if we make that our intention. As an activist and astrologer, Caroline W. Casey once said, "The invisible world would like to help. But spiritual etiquette requires that we ask whether we call this prayer or making an intention." The essential point is that it's a process of questioning, receiving, and commitment. It's about creating a purpose for ourselves and whatever we might call our higher power. And it's not that God doesn't know what you want or need; spiritual etiquette says we must ask for what we want. Caroline's book, *Making the Gods Work for You,* is a helpful book for understanding this concept.

THE TOOL

Laughter provides a full-scale workout for muscles and provides a rush of stress-busting endorphins. Since our bodies cannot distinguish between a real or fake laugh, your laughing will positively impact us. You do not need to be happy or have a sense of humor to receive help from a good belly laugh. Just start laughing. Be careful, it is contagious, and soon everyone may be laughing.

Laughter is an excellent way to reduce fear in our lives and help us cope with and survive a stressful lifestyle. Of course, it will not change what you're going through, but it will change your mental perspective of the situation and be less stressful. The essence of using fear as a tool for positive results and releasing stuck energy in the blue chakra will take a problematic situation and transform it with positive energy.

Breath-work is a much-used primary tool to dissolve fear. I use breathwork and a visualization exercise to find the tension and anxiety of any relatives who show up to steal my moment. Reducing fear and its physical manifestations will open us to new and more incredible accomplishments. Harnessing our fear for our use can be the first step in achieving our goals. Just think of what you could do if you were not afraid.

Take note of when you feel afraid and where you feel the throat, the gut.

Notice when you move away from your fear.

Notice when you move closer to your fear.

Invite your fears to tea and having that uncomfortable talk and release the energy that blocks your blue chakra. It is a good thing.

Do this right now. Please take a deep breath, and as you breathe, notice the way your breath feels in your body. Close your eyes and rest your palms on your knees to receive the flow. Relax your jaw and take a big inhale through your mouth. Notice your breath as it travels down your throat and into your lungs. As you breathe, feel the muscles in your shoulders relax. Feel the muscles in your face relax. Focus on your inhale. Your body will naturally exhale. Keep your inhale and your exhale connected. Breathe. Do this regularly and often for relaxation.

Fear and its many manifestations are the roots of important and challenging issues. The more we can understand and transform our fears, the more we can do with much less effort.

I am leaving you with a gift—John 14:27, "Peace I leave with you; my peace I give you. I do not give to you as the world gives. Do not let your hearts be troubled, and do not be afraid."

Nailah G. Beraki ND, LMHC, Ph.D., believes in a holistic business coaching mindset strategy that equals results. She is a Reiki Master and owner of Shakeray Wellness Collaborative, LLC.

With over four decades of experience, her compassion, humor, and earthy approach allow her to help others make a positive difference in their lives and help others. Her ability to empower others has gained her the description of 'transformational.'

Nailah integrates business strategy marketing and money mindset strategy. Building a business will feel profound and transformative as well as profitable. You are increasing your skills, expertise, the beliefs that define you. Business growth is self-growth; we remove the shame limiting beliefs that are not good enough. The elements to do business and personal development go hand in hand. You cannot develop your business without developing yourself. You're going to have to take on the self-growth and responsibility to earn the freedom of being a business owner.

www.nailahberaki.com

nailahberaki@gmail.com

CHAPTER 20

IMPACT, INFLUENCE, SUCCESS

BUILDING A POWERFUL NETWORK

Anna Pereira

"If you want to go fast, go alone.
If you want to go far, go together."

~African proverb

MY STORY

Happy people. Successful people. Content people. Ambitious people. Confident people. Humble people. Respected people. Influential people. Change agents—impact makers. I like to be around these folks! I also hope to be considered a peer.

The phone rang. "Hello? How are you! How have you been? Oh really? Interesting. That's great. I'm so happy for you. Yes, I know someone (more conversation). Okay. I'll get back to you." He hung up the phone. He dialed.

"Hey, how are you? I just got off the phone with (insert name); he will be (insert activity/project) and is looking to (find someone, do something). What are you doing these days?"

I cocked my head to the side. I heard the authentic, centered, thoughtful, integrity-based strategic connector who later became my husband on the phone with his friends.

I found this astonishing! He was called. He picked up, with no hesitation or vacillating. No, *do I want to take this call?* And he hung up, placed a call, and *they* picked up. Wow. No waiting. No playing tag or ego games.

Most of Hugo's network are friends. He aligns himself with high achievers who are good people doing great things.

I was curious, energized, and inspired by his relationship skills and prestigious network. People reached out to him with opportunities and requests, and he knew exactly who to call for a connection he sought.

Hugo is a genuine, heart-centered connector and an expert in his field.

It was very new to me and lit me up! Like a brick over my head, I realized, *hmph! It's not what you know; it's who you know.* This suddenly made *real* sense to me but in a very authentic, not just strategic, way.

You hear these sayings and think it applies to others, but it's true for ourselves. We work on gaining credentials, education, wisdom, and tools to operate in our work—building a website, creating content, buying inventory—thinking these essentials will lead to success. At the end of the day, these are all things that can change, be replaced, or mutate and shift as we find new interests, skills, and more.

What can we count on to consistently be there to fortify any life experience or challenge, celebrate, or call out for support? People—good, solid, heart-centered people.

People of their word.

People who know people.

People who care.

People you want to be there for to support as well.

Doers. Movers. Shakers. Steady. Trusting. Reliable. Investable. Those who are there for you and those you'd be there for.

Relationships are an investment. More than money, relationships take equity that has no measure. Our investment is rare and valuable to us, and what we can't get back; time, heart, emotion.

Until I witnessed how he navigated conversations with interest, curiosity, and integrity, I had a very different experience with relationships.

I don't know if I ever put intention into relationships. Either I met people through school, shared interests, or work that led to the passing of time with those people, or they were filling a need. Most of my relationships were UN-intentional.

I had great friends and was a great friend, but relationships were more transactional, and (for many) if they weren't serving me, I abandoned them.

Maybe, if I had seen my worth and value sooner and learned how to see others through self-love and discernment, I may have had much more success, joy, fulfillment, and ease sooner.

I felt alone, different, and separate at the end of my days. Many relationships were shallow. To think of some of the people I allowed to occupy time and space in my life and heart leaves me with a sour taste and a bit of 'pity on me.'

I had leverage to keep people around; I worked hard, showed up, was in the 'beautiful people circle' but when it came down to it, who was truly there for me and my best interests?

Did I have someone to call who would bail me out of jail? Thank goodness this never happened!

Did I have someone I could completely confide in and trust to advise me wisely, without judgment, through a challenging time?

Did I have someone who'd always pick up the phone when I called?

Did I have someone who'd support my dream(s)?

Did I have someone who wouldn't judge me, my dreams or aspirations, and share encouraging words?

Did I have someone to count on to walk my dog if I went on vacation?

Did I have someone to trust to hold a key to my house?

If I dig deeper and had someone for each of these things, could I see them doing that in five or ten years?

Are they in my life for a reason, season, or lifetime?

And more importantly, am I that person for someone?

I hope so.

Who are they?

I hope people see me as a trustworthy, genuine, integrity-based, honest person and friend. But I, too, should take inventory of who in my life I'd step up for. And in what way? And why?

Why do I have _____ in my life? This is an important question.

"I have to go to Spain in a few days."

"Well, how will that affect your green card status? You aren't supposed to leave the country for two years."

"You will have to join me."

My head spun. We were married only six months prior, and I had no plans of leaving New Jersey, let alone the country! *My husband is going to leave!* I felt like a military wife, and Hugo just got called back into active duty.

"The Sheikh is buying the club, and I have to go to help them."

Malaga Spain. Good thing I had a passport! Malaga is a beautiful place. The south of Spain, adjacent to the posh Marbella where the rich and privileged frolic—beaches, dining, ambiance—paradise.

"But I don't want you to go. Do you really have to leave?"

There I went again, thinking of my needs and holes, not of the bigger picture.

All of his work and life's experience led up to an extraordinary opportunity. And I was selfish and potentially sabotaging our relationship if I showed up needy and fearful.

One can only dream of such an opportunity to restructure a first division soccer team, which became champions by his contribution and expertise. His expertise helped create millions in revenue for the club and success for us.

This was all because of his relationships. Someone heard of an opportunity and called *him*. He fosters solid, powerful relationships.

I was starting to get it. I needed to be on his team in our relationship. His success was my success too. I needed to:

- Trust him
- Have self-love
- Embody self-sovereignty
- Be a better cheerleader

Six months into a marriage, after an eight-week dating period, he's packing to leave the country and not return. I tried to wrap my head around moving abroad soon after. It was a whirlwind, and I was scared.

Our first date was October 26, 2009, and we were married on December 23, 2009. I knew he was the one and acted fast! If you're curious about how I got to be so lucky, in my book, *The Wellness Universe Guide to Complete Self-Care, 25 Tools for Happiness*, I share how I manifested my magnificent husband.

My journey took a serious looking-at. Up-leveling who I thought I was, who I project myself as, and who I want to be started getting clear.

If I continued down the road of selfish, fear-based, self-absorbed, self-motivated, "What have I got to gain from this person or relationship?" then I'd suffocate it and lose it altogether.

Who was my husband to me? What had I seen in him that made me say he is extraordinary, different, the *one*!?

I needed to step up and up-level myself to be the person for him, and for myself, I needed to be. This would be the only way anything would ever change in my life.

Finding heart-centered value in myself helped me to:

- Create boundaries
- Trust my intuition
- Evaluate situations from a power source rather than fear
- Take action that fed my soul and my life success
- Genuinely appreciate others

This was all very important because I didn't want to lose the best thing that ever entered my life. My soiree with countless low vibration people taught me how much to appreciate good, solid, real love.

But I knew, "Your vibe attracts your tribe!" Even though I mentally, emotionally, and spiritually upgraded myself, I wasn't at the level I needed to be, or I wouldn't feel the way I felt.

I was very blessed and grateful for my relationship!

Because of my successful relationship with the man of my dreams, you'll hear me reference him as *My Prince*. I was inspired to be a better version of myself which allowed me to attract and surround myself with higher vibration people, live the life of my dreams, travel the world (even during COVID), and live the best life experiences with great success.

Where has this all led, aside from my personal life being a parade of blessings? Building a platform and community many said couldn't be done.

The vision for The Wellness Universe was always a resource for people seeking wellness to find those who can help them to better their lives. I believe a happy, healthy, healed human leads to world peace. We in The Wellness Universe all believe this and work in our purpose to make this a reality.

My ability to foster great relationships has led to my success.

With more than 100 independent recommendations on Linkedin from those who've worked with me, and countless collaborations and partnerships, you can believe it's more than what I know that has helped me achieve success.

THE TOOL

In full transparency, I'm not a relationship coach. I'm sharing my perspective based on my real-life experiences based on the outcome of building a large community and many wonderful relationships.

Benefits I've experienced from positive, fulfilling relationships:

- Emotional support
- Empowers your purpose

- Amplifies your message
- Supports your goals
- Gives you inspiration
- You never feel alone
- Allows you to share your love

Building strong, solid relationships requires knowing who you are, knowing your worth, and valuing yourself from a heart-centered space. This helps you share who you are authentically and receive the other person's greatest self and all the goodness they offer.

When we come from a place of lack, fear, and unworthiness, we set ourselves up for failed relationships, over-giving, being taken advantage of, or being manipulative to fill a hole.

We've all heard, "You're the average of the five people you spend the most time with," a quote attributed most often to motivational speaker Jim Rohn. I don't believe this. It's everyone in your network and those who you haven't even met yet that influence you.

You will attract people through:

- Your reputation
- Your service
- Your talents
- Your needs and more

Fostering real relationships that reciprocate mutually beneficial fulfillment—emotionally, mentally, and financially—is foundational to your well-being and long-term success and good fortune.

Relationships we keep pouring into without receiving anything uplifting in return, drain us and suck us dry. Beyond that, they literally **keep you from your highest success and most wonderful life experience.**

That is a grim reality.

If you can think of relationships as partnerships, you can evaluate and turn on the power in your network.

Ask yourself:

- Can I trust this person?
- Have they shown up for me?
- Are they excited for me?
- What is the reputation of this person?
- Do they appreciate me?

Then ask yourself:

- Can they trust in me?
- Would I show up for them?
- Am I genuinely excited about their dreams, goals, and successes?
- Do I embody confidence and have a good name?
- Do I appreciate them?

As you seek to encircle yourself with talented, trusting, dependable people, you must be willing to be all that as well.

For those you've identified to fill the first set of questions with a positive response, are you that person for them?

Be honest. You should want to be that stellar human in return. It's a great feeling to want to show up and support someone. If you don't feel this way, a re-evaluation of the relationship may be in order.

Spend your time with those that light you up and whom you wish to mirror. That is keeping great company!

CHECK YOUR ENERGY

Day to day, no matter how much self-work we do, environmental factors, stress, other's actions, and decisions play a role in how we feel and can potentially impact how we act. It's human nature.

It's important to check your energy and honor your core values that help you show up in all your magnificence (leadership) and adhere to your boundaries (self-love, self-sovereignty).

I used to get so frustrated when I allowed someone to let me down. I had very high expectations. I took it personally. After similar scenarios played out over and over, I assessed it wasn't that they were letting *me* down; they were falling short of the potential I saw in them. Now, I create opportunities and see how someone shows up to set my expectations accordingly.

Maybe something came up. Maybe they just didn't think it was important to apply themselves. Maybe they're lacking awareness or confidence. Whatever the reason, I just make a note and know how to invest myself into that relationship going forward.

After all, if you allowed someone to babysit your child and they fell asleep, and your child wandered out of the house, would you have them back?

We must honor each time we extend our trust and allow someone to take a position requiring responsibility within our life. We need to hold them accountable, yet the awareness of our expectations is vital for harmony.

ATTRACTING THE BEST RELATIONSHIPS

Who are you showing up as? What are you offering? I'm much more inspired to connect with someone if they offer rather than ask.

What does that mean?

I get approached a lot. Many people see what I've created and want in. I disdain people who want to fleece my community (I'm very protective, and Wellness Universe members are like family to me). I don't entertain those who show up with 'a great solution for me or my business' before getting to know me or what I do! That amuses me. Imagine a doctor saying, "I can cure you!" and you haven't even shared what's wrong yet?

Connecting on a human level, being curious, asking about their goals, finding commonalities, being honest, vulnerable, and sharing your humanness goes a long way.

Create an environment where someone feels seen and heard, not sold to.

BE YOURSELF

Puff, fluff, and faking it 'til you make it have no place in building a real relationship. You can't be someone else for an extended period. You'll feel empty, exhausted, and unable to keep it up. And if you're involved in this practice, it may be to fill a void of your own. More self-care and self-work are needed.

Drop into your heart-space and let your heart speak. If you believe in who you are and what you do, and take full ownership of your responsibilities, actions, and outcomes, showing up authentically will be the result.

What is your why, personally and professionally?

Who will support you to live in your why with bliss?

Maybe it's time to reevaluate current relationships. Maybe it's time to seek out new ones.

A once a year relationship inventory is a great practice.

PEOPLE WILL FORGET WHAT YOU DID, BUT THEY REMEMBER HOW YOU MADE THEM FEEL

I'm paraphrasing the great Maya Angelou with that header.

Got extraordinary people in your igloo? Always share your gratitude and appreciation for them. I still tell my husband 'Thank you' when he pays for dinner, which is always!

Without a specific reason, appreciate someone today! Two powerful, simple ways to uplift someone I care about:

Through words: I let those around me know they're appreciated for all they do and **all they are.**

Through influence-building actions: I share my experiences working with people with my networks. I give them influence and shout them out.

QUICK INSPIRATIONS

In what ways can you empower your connections?

- Write them a recommendation on LinkedIn or another reputable platform. This is *much more* powerful than just a social media plug. It can be used on their website or when other potential clients are researching them. It's a powerful gift that takes just a few minutes.

- Send a thank you card or note of appreciation or a small gift! Hey, how about sharing **this book** with someone as a transformational gift? I also like to send handmade items and my favorite things like milk-frothers, to say thanks! BONUS: Can you send a gift of appreciation or congratulations that comes from **someone else in your network**? That's a relationship-building two-fer!

- Text someone you haven't connected with in a while to say hello, send them love or offer to catch up.

- Can you refer your connections to each other? Sweet! You're in the relationship-building big leagues now.

Big network or small, it's all about quality.

Every single human has the power to change the world. We cannot do it alone. Be with those who power you up, amplify your joy, and who you're excited to support, share, and be in the company of.

We who have divine relationships are truly blessed. We all have the power to create this! We're supported and never feel alone when we keep the right company and are the best company for those we treasure, value, and love. This makes us all unstoppable!

Anna Pereira is the CEO and Head Goddess of The Wellness Universe and CEO of Soul Ventures, a woman-owned business, where her mission is to make the world a better place. She's an inspirational leader, mentor, and connector for business owners who are changing the world. As an author and creator of wellness events, projects, and programs, Anna is an expert at showcasing, promoting, and supporting the world's most talented wellness professionals.

Anna lives between Europe and her birthplace, New Jersey, USA, with her husband, sports expert, and investor, Hugo Varela. The couple has adopted pets (one dog and two cats) and cares for strays. Big Red, their African Gray, loves to speak English and Portuguese and is the ruler of the house. When time allows, Anna enjoys turning on the creative flow by painting, writing, and creating custom T-shirts and jewelry. Finding balance in nature or at the beach with friends is her joy. She's dedicated to serving her calling and leaving her legacy as a 'conduit for change' by bringing more health, happiness, and well-being to the world with a collaborative spirit and intentional action. Learn more about Anna and The Wellness Universe at TheWellnessUniverse.com

https://www.thewellnessuniverse.com/world-changers/annapereira/

CHAPTER 21

FEARLESS

BORN TO WIN

Kearn Crockett Cherry

MY STORY

We are all born in the beginning without fear. If you think about the babies who climb from the bed with no fear of falling, they literally learn from watching. Children are naturally more resilient than adults. They take risks with unforeseen consequences. Everything is fine until the world starts focusing on the danger or the impossibilities. We're born with the opportunity to win at anything. Our environment and surroundings are what tell us that everything is possible. Then the people in our environment tell us something different.

As a middle child, I always felt safe around my siblings. I often felt challenged to do more, either from watching my older sister or just trying to keep up with my younger brother, who was always a top student in school. There are five of us, and we were all more academically inclined to excel. I look back now and realize it was more natural for us. Just imagine if my mom, who worked two jobs, was able to stay home and focus on pushing us to greatness. Going to grade school was never an issue. She didn't have to tell us to make As; we just did. I now look back and realize that I didn't really have fear in those days. I was surrounded by people who loved me and always made sure I was taken care of. As kids, we don't realize how close danger really is and how simple choices will change our lives forever.

As a young lady and teenager, I began to make some mistakes that eventually changed my life. Being naive can eventually catch up with you. I found myself pregnant in my senior year of high school and not able to focus on the good grades that seemed to come so naturally before. I realized I wouldn't go off to college as previously planned. The days of just being young and free were over. I now had someone else to worry about. I would be responsible for making sure he was fed and clothed. I had to assure him he wouldn't have to fear anything because I would be there for him. I found a way to continue pressing forward and go to college, but fear found its way into my life. It would be there daily. Instead of just going to college, I now had to work, go to school, then come home and care for my son.

Life reminded me that it's the choices I made that introduced fear. As long as we're successful, we move ahead full steam, but if there's a roadblock or change, we tend to doubt things and allow fear to creep in. It then becomes about how to handle fear in the moments when you're not sure about your next move, step, or decision. I mentioned before that I decided to press forward. I had a three-week-old son to take care of, but I still needed to go to college. I chose to change my career field to something allowing more flexibility. Basically, I want to always be able to work and provide for my family. This would start my journey in the medical field.

I went on to marry my son's father. I joined him in Germany, then Arizona. Through all of that, I was determined to finish my nursing degree. Together my husband and I would embark on a journey that required nothing more than guts. Once we landed in Arizona with three little ones under seven, my husband found himself quickly out of the Army. We landed in what I referred to then as "Nowhere Land," Sierra Vista. Back then, there was nothing for a budding family and finding work outside of the military was almost impossible, even in the medical field. We were determined; we never gave up; an opportunity in the medical field opened. Unfortunately, finishing college became a struggle. It felt like the door was closing, and there were no other options. *God will always make a way.*

We struggled for a while in that town and finally started looking outside of Sierra Vista. Life has a way of helping you understand that what you think at the time is for the worst is actually for the better. Several of us had started talking about driving an hour and a half to get into nursing school there. My husband and I were tired but knew we had to make some changes. We took the plunge and joined forces with a few friends who worked with us at a nursing home. Though we did not find an opening for nursing, we found a medical school that offered occupational therapy. Did I mention earlier that it was an hour and a half drive? Or that we had three little ones to raise? We knew the risk was high, and we had no idea how to make it happen. We had no family nearby, but we knew life had to change. So we took the leap of faith.

This journey would not be without lots of struggles. The five of us had to become a team on a fearless mission to change our lives for the better. I didn't even realize if I was in Sierra Vista or Tucson many days. During all this craziness, I started working in Tucson. So some days, instead of carpooling home, I would stay and work overnight. There were so many roadblocks. My husband and I lost our car. Another car died on the interstate, and the last had no air conditioning to fight the Arizona heat. We struggled with getting there every day, and our classmates became like the enemy you just wish would disappear forever. I'm sure our kids must have thought we were insane, but eventually, they would see better days. Sometimes you have to run through fear—face it head-on to accomplish your mission. You have to be fearless to be successful.

My husband and I learned from that experience that no one would hand you success. You have to take it. We had to stare fear in the face and move through it. Fear will always be around to challenge you and push you to be your best self. The bible says that you will experience trials and tribulations, but it didn't say you would fail. My husband and I finished that school and have been in the home care business for 25 years. We don't allow anyone to tell us what we can't do. We do what needs to be done. You realize everyone is set up to win at some point in life, but that doesn't mean you won't be challenged or approached by fear. When you push through, success awaits you on the other side!

THE TOOL

How to operate in the Fearless Zone

1. Stop caring about what others think. Most people aren't even thinking about you. They really only care about themselves. So focus on what matters to you. You will not be able to please everyone. It's okay to focus on *you*.

2. Operate in your gifts and talents. First, figure out what your gifts are. Identifying what you're called to do, you should operate in your genius zone. If you're not sure what your purpose is, pray on it. Proverbs 18:16: "A man's gifts will make room for him and sit at the table of great men." People who work in their gifts are fearless.

3. Be curious. Always be willing to learn and improve your skills and talents. The people who are the best at what they do are always curious enough to ask questions and seek advice from others.

4. Be accountable. Sometimes your greatest enemy is looking right back at you in the mirror. You should always take time to self-reflect and work on being self-aware. Once you own your mistake, make a plan to stop it from continuing to happen and then act on it. This takes humility, but it will feel so rewarding in the end.

5. Take one step at a time. Take smaller steps toward your goals. Goals can sometimes feel overwhelming. Break them down into smaller, manageable tasks. When you do this, it will help you build up the confidence to accomplish your goals.

6. Get excited about the possibilities. Stop thinking about what could go wrong and start focusing on everything that can go right. See the end results first and then pray on it.

7. Step out of your comfort zone. Do you ever wonder why some athletes are called champions and others are called exceptional? Champions tend to raise their skills to another level while under extreme pressure. Even in practice, they're always trying something new to improve their skills. To be a champion, you must stretch yourself beyond your limits. It takes an unusual amount of determination to operate

at this level, but the rewards are worth it. Champions understand that fear is just part of the process, and their goal is to conquer it.

8. Go ahead and fail. If you're not failing at something, then you're not taking enough risk. Failures are a part of growth. I've started many businesses that failed and closed, but it allowed me to learn something new. I was able to take away the positive things that went right and learn from the things that went wrong. It can be hard to face your failure, but it's essential to the process of facing fear.

9. Be careful who you allow to whisper in your ears. Surround yourself with positive people. There are people in your inner circle that you need to release. Some people enter your life for a season, and when they stay too long, they can start holding you back. There are times when we're in relationships that require us to manage it because of our obligations, but that doesn't mean that the person has to remain in your inner circle. Your inner circle is that small group of people who you check in with. Some are what we like to call your "ride or die" friends, but even those need to be re-evaluated. Negative energy can be the catalyst to destruction.

10. Be over-prepared. There's an old saying, "practice makes perfect." Practicing actually helps to reduce anxiety and improve your confidence. I often tell my clients: If you're going to be speaking on stage, make sure you take the time to prepare. It could be as simple as writing your presentation down, reading it aloud, and then recording it. Sometimes being scared is directly related to being unprepared.

11. Procrastination equals fear. Procrastination can be associated with the fear of winning. Stop waiting for tomorrow. It may never happen if you wait until tomorrow. Procrastination can be very paralyzing. You have to practice pushing yourself to do things on time or even early.

12. Be you! Don't try to be someone else. We are all unique individuals. It's much easier to just do you. It's okay that everyone doesn't like you. When you're being sincere, you'll find it is less stressful. Believe in yourself. You are enough.

13. Be confident. First, work on changing your mindset. Your beliefs and attitude can impact your ability to be confident. People who lack self-confidence are more likely not to be successful. Building confidence requires you to make changes in your life. It's okay to hire a mindset coach as well.

14. Stay focused. This is essential to success, but it's also important to be fearless. A focused mind is rarely stopped by fear. Focused individuals are typically driven and determined to achieve their goals at all costs. They set their goals and push through anything standing in their way. They may even find a need to pivot, but they never let a challenge keep them from their mission and achieving their goals. They literally become fearless and unstoppable!

Kearn Crockett Cherry

"Butts in the Seats Queen"

kearn@prnhomecareservices.com

www.kearncherry.com

Speaker, 13-time #1 bestselling author, and award-winning businesswoman **Kearn Crockett Cherry** is a female tycoon with a "leg-up" in successful entrepreneurship. Laying to rest any stigma surrounding the stagnancy of female leadership in the deep south, Kearn has enjoyed more than two decades of excellence as the CEO of a thriving health care business on the Gulf Coast of Mississippi.

Kearn hosts a portfolio holding countless awards, acknowledging her abilities; locally, nationally, and internationally. She is a recognized figure in both business and communal leadership, holding membership and chair positions on diverse councils and local organizations.

The Success Women's Conference is an award winning-business leadership conference attracting an annual audience of over 17,000 attendees worldwide. Kearn Cherry and her contributing partners have a reputation for revolutionizing the way women interpret both public speaking and business on a global scale. She is also the creator of **Power Up Summit** and **Level Up Summit**.

In 2001, Kearn Cherry effortlessly graced the pages of one of the most popular publications in the world, **Essence Magazine**. Featured in both their local and international publications, Kearn was recognized as the "**Comeback Queen**," confirming her commitment to exemplify dynamic business agility. Today, Kearn is a familiar face on several Magazine covers. Recently featured on **Black Enterprise, VIP Magazine, Speakers Magazine, Sheen Magazine**, and her very own, her favorites.

Giving birth to an Amazon #1 bestselling book, *Trailblazers Who Lead: Unsung Heroes*, a manuscript comprising 29 stories featuring several well-respected female entrepreneurs, moguls, and business professionals.

Enthusiastic about the future, Kearn remains diligent in helping entrepreneurs reach their destined potential. She recently released her #1 bestseller, *Make It Happen* anthology, with 30 authors. In addition, she is the visionary for *Trailblazers Who Lead II* and her new anthology, *Undefeated*, 100 women sharing their secrets to winning.

CHAPTER 22

STAND OUT, BE HEARD, AND SHINE BRIGHT

HOW TO CREATE A BRAND FROM SCRATCH

Dr. Pam Perry

.

MY STORY

"Wow, I see your name everywhere." That's what I often hear from people I've met who've seen my social media, read my blog, heard my podcast, picked up my magazine, seen me on TV, or even attended some virtual events where I was presenting.

In full transparency, I'm a publicist, working with top brands for over 25 years, from corporations to nonprofits, and recently with authors and speakers. During my career, I've been the PR director for The Salvation Army, worked in an agency as the lead publicist for Dunkin' Donuts and McDonald's, and have had contracts to create PR and social media campaigns for the Detroit Area Agency of Aging, AARP, and The Charles H. Wright Museum of African American History.

I have brand recognition today not just because of my public relations skills, hard work, and consistency but also because I've connected to the right people. They've brought up my name in rooms. They've nominated me for awards I won. They've made me aware of many opportunities that have been life-changing. They've helped me crack the code so I could accelerate my brand, which has helped build my business and save me time.

Yes, getting out there is hard work, and it's necessary when building a brand, but it's not what sustains you. It's all about connecting with the right people to keep opportunities flowing and your business growing.

You might not know this about me, but magazines are one of my favorite things in life. They are full of stories about people who have done amazing things. When magazines come out with new articles, it makes me feel like anything is possible for myself and for others!

Some magazines even allow readers to write their own articles if they have something important to share. Magazines (online or print) also give the public a chance to voice their opinion through letters to the editor. In addition, magazines position your brand as influential.

Speakers Magazine, the magazine I've published for five years, has done amazing things for those I've featured on the covers and for those who've written articles. For example, one cover girl was featured on Fox Soul TV and sold out her event because of the additional exposure.

Another cover story distributed the magazines on the tables at an event he was speaking at, and he told me, "My stock went up." Meaning that he was perceived as a "celebrity" speaker to the audience because he was on the cover of a national magazine, and they were reading about him before he even said one word from the stage. He said people began booking him for events way in advance because he was seen as an "in-demand" speaker. That's how PR works.

The writers of Speakers magazine have gotten business too. One, in particular, won a $5,000 contract to write website copy by having a consistent voice via articles in the magazine showcasing her expertise; this is what gained the trust of the prospect, which turned into a really good client.

If you want to be seen and heard so you can have an impact on the world, I will outline the steps I've found that will help you build a brand, from scratch.

THE TOOL

DECIDE WHAT YOU REALLY WANT

The first step is to decide what you really want to accomplish by being seen and heard. Note, it's not for your ego. Think about what you want to be known for. Be very intentional about this because your brand is everything that speaks up about who you are or what service or product your business provides. It doesn't matter if it's newspapers, podcasts, publicity campaigns, speeches. Whatever it is, make sure there's an intention behind all of them!

Then, you need to establish your credibility. If there is anything that can damage your brand at all, ask yourself how it will affect the trust of the people who are reading about what you have to say. Is everything in line with being credible, or do some things seem out-of-place? Do a quick Google check on your name. What pops up on page one? Do your social media platforms need scrubbing? Do you need to do a clean-up on your website to reflect how you want to be seen?

You can also write articles or guest blogs for other credible sites. This will help you showcase your expertise.

MAKE IT ALL ABOUT THEM

Are you ready to say goodbye to all the frustration and lost time searching for media contacts and scripting the perfect pitch? Let me share with you how to create, cultivate, nurture relationships with media professionals. But first, adopt this mindset; the media is in business to make money. They make money from advertising. Advertising comes from having an audience. The larger the audience, the more money the media outlet can charge.

Journalists have a job. They need sources for stories. They need industry experts just like you. Your job is to help them find you and to get them to trust you. And when you gain their trust, they'll reach out to you often because they know you'd be a good source for their stories.

In other words, make it all about them. Start thinking about how you can make it all about their audience. What do they want? How can you help them? The journalist has two sets of people to please, their boss and their audience. They make their bosses happy by delivering a great story that helps, entertains, inspires, informs, or educates the audience (readers, listeners, or viewers).

WHERE TO FIND THE MEDIA (FOR FREE)

1. *Twitter.* If you're not on Twitter, you're missing out. The media loves Twitter. It's one of the best places to find out what a reporter is talking about and what they may be interested in. Remember, it's all about them, not you. Follow your favorite journalists and see if you resonate with them. Retweet them. Most have their own personal websites listed as well as their email on their profiles for "news tips."

2. *Linkedin.* This is my favorite social media platform. I love Linkedin because you can connect with journalists and see their career history. This is a great place to understand who the journalists, producers, or editors are. Of course, you have to request to connect with them, but it's simple to do. I have over 10,000 media contacts on Linkedin. One service I provide for clients is showing them how to find and connect with media.

3. *Muckrack.* This is a publicist and journalists tool, but anyone can use it. I love this online directory because it lists all the journalists' last stories, tweets, and online contact information. There is a paid version and a free version, but the free version is fine if you're just starting out. It's a great way to double-check and verify more contact information that you may find on Twitter or Linkedin.

THE MEDIA PITCH

In order to build your brand from scratch, media is key! Most people think that branding is all about creating a catchy logo and slapping it on everything. While this is part of it, successful branding goes much deeper than that. Your brand needs to be visible everywhere your customers are looking, and you need to create a consistent message across all channels. This includes social media, your website, email marketing, and more.

It would help if you were also strategic about pitching your brand to the media. Pitching the wrong story or angle can ruin your chances of getting publicity, so it's important to know what reporters are looking for. In general, they're looking for stories that are unique, interesting, and relevant to their audience.

When you're pitching your story, make sure to include the answers to these questions:

- Why should they care? (What's in it for them?)
- Who is this relevant to? (Who are their readers/viewers?)
- What makes this stand out from other brands and products like yours?
- How does it fit into current trends in the news or in your industry?

If you can answer these questions and package your story in an appealing way, the media will be more likely to take notice. And when they do, it will increase your brand's visibility and help you stand out from the competition. So don't wait any longer; start branding like a superstar.

BUT…BE HUMBLE, ASK FOR HELP

Remember that it's okay not to know how to do something. In this information-driven world we live in, most people are just one Youtube or online course behind what you know. Everything changes so fast, so there is no way to know everything.

Be humble, ask questions, ask for help. Find a mentor or hire a coach. Mentors open doors, and coaches shorten your learning curve. My mentors have recommended that I appear on national shows like The Word Network, PBS and speak at major industry events at the Book Expo of America during the Publishing University.

Asking for help is never easy, but it can be the best thing you do for yourself. PR mentors and coaches are public relations experts that will guide you through the media maze. They provide support by asking questions about your pitch and providing you with contact information or suggestions on how to find them.

There are many public relations professionals who have had success in their careers and would be happy to help you with your public relations needs. If you're struggling, reach out to someone for assistance. Many times people feel that they need to do everything themselves, but it's important to ask for help when we need it!

CREATE A MIND MAP

Mind mapping is a simple but powerful tool for creating a detailed to-do list for achieving your goals. I think mind-mapping is better than a vision board, but I do recommend both!

A mind map lets you determine what information you need, who you'll need to talk to, what steps you need to take, what deadlines you'll need to meet, and so on, for each and every PR and branding goal.

When I teach my clients in my Branding Accelerator program how to reach their branding goals, I use mind mapping to help them "chunk down" their big goals into individual talks. It's like how a person eats an elephant, one bite at a time.

MIND-MAPPING STEPS

1. Center circle: In the center circle, jot down the name of your goal. For instance, "Get local media attention"

2. Outside circles: Next, divide the goal into major categories of tasks you'll need to complete to accomplish your greater goal, like local TV stations, radio shows, daily newspapers, and weekly newspapers.

3. Spokes: Then, draw spokes radiating outward from each mini-circle and label each one (such as Twitter, Linkedin, Muckrack contacts of each person that works at the corresponding media outlet).

On a separate line connected to the mini-circle, write every single step you need to take to engage, meet and pitch to the media professional. Break down each one of the more detailed task spokes with action items to help you create your master outreach schedule.

MAKE A DAILY OUTREACH SCHEDULE

Reaching out to people is key to building a brand from start to finish. I remember reaching out to several people in my industry when I first started my business. They were hosting conferences, and I asked if I could help by volunteering in any capacity. They immediately said yes, and they could watch me in action. The next year, I was a speaker. I presented: "How to Promote Your Book," and positioned myself as an expert.

Once you've completed your mind map for your goal, convert all of the to-do items into daily action items by listing each one on your daily to-do lists and committing to a completion date for each one. Then schedule them in the appropriate order into your calendar and do whatever it takes to stay on schedule.

Think of it this way; you are one contact away from building the brand of your dreams.

Now go take some action. Bust through the fear, be brave. You have within you the power to make your dreams come true. You just have to stay focused, make the connections and follow through.

Need some help in developing your personal PR Plan? Download my free ebook, *"Be Heard, Stand Out and Get Known,"* at PamPerryPR.com/ebook.

Who is **Dr. Pam Perry**? The *Detroit Free Press* called her a "marketing whiz on almost an immortal mission." *Publishers Weekly* refers to her as a "PR Guru" - but most know her as the "PR Angel."

Founder of Blacks in Advertising, Radio & Television (BART), The National Association of Black Podcasters & the Chocolate Pages Network, Perry serves as a goldmine of information, connections, and transformation. Her signature program is offered twice a year, The Branding Accelerator.

Dr. Perry serves as the CEO of Ministry Marketing Solutions, her public relations consulting firm, where she takes authors' works from vision to manifestation. She helps them position, package, and promote their brand, and get bookings for speaking engagements.

This multi-award-winning entrepreneur speaks, writes, consults, and coaches on marketing, branding, and public relations. She loves coaching clients to be "Red Carpet" ready and brand like a superstar.

Download her free ebook on "How to Get Out There and Be Heard" at pamperrypr.com/ebook.

CLOSING CHAPTER

Unstoppable while being fierce, fearless, and unf*ckawithable in life and business was born from the realization that women need intelligent tools based on real wisdom they can tap into to obtain insight, guidance, knowledge, and motivation to keep moving forward on their journey toward bliss.

Unstoppable's goal is to inspire, empower, encourage, and ignite the fire that's needed to allow one to push beyond the limits of their capacity and do all they came into the world to achieve, no matter what!

My desire for this book is that it becomes the "go-to" resource to obtain the words of wisdom that guide the future generations of females to fulfill their purpose and achieve their greatness despite the challenges that may come upon them. Most importantly, to support other women in doing the same in a spirit of empowerment, harmony, and unity.

"Females are the most powerful species on the planet, and when we come together, we are a force to behold. We are unstoppable!"

~Rochel Marie Lawson

When I began gathering my thoughts of how I wanted to put this book together, I wanted to make sure the information contained in the text represented actual challenges that women face on their journey to being Unf*ckwithable. I wanted to make sure that the stories written in the book painted a picture of a fundamental challenge and the catalyst that made moving beyond the challenge obtainable.

I wanted the stories to be heartfelt and relatable to all women. I desired the book to represent women worldwide and show that no matter what country we may reside in, we all face similar challenges in life.

As this book came together and the authors began discussing their stories with me, I knew that this book would go beyond just being words of wisdom and guidance. This book allows the authors' legacy of understanding and enlightenment to be passed on to their daughters, granddaughters, and great-granddaughters. I knew that this would be the perfect book for this moment in our lives.

"Life was meant to be lived and curiosity must be kept alive. One must never, for whatever reason, turn one's back on life."

~Eleanor Roosevelt

Unstoppable: Be Fierce, Fearless and Unf*ckwithable in Life and Business is a book that is a must-read for all woman starting at the age of 16. It's a book you should share with every women in your life. It contains timeless logic and heartfelt stories laced with laughter. This book written for the 21st century will transcend beyond this time.

It is my wish that you reach out and connect with the authors, share how what they wrote in the book resonated with you, obtain their gifts, follow them on social media and join us at one of the Brave, Bold & Unstoppable Women's Summits.™

https://www.unstoppable-womens-summit.com.

I am grateful to you for allowing me to occupy time in your day. Thank you for buying, reading and sharing this book. Thank you for being a part of my journey and allowing me to be a part of yours.

You now have an understanding of the importance of sharing our stories and how the wisdom we obtain from these stories give us the power and strength to move forward on our path to bliss.

I am grateful to you for being Unstoppable while being Fierce, Fearless & Unf*ckwithable in Life and Business!

Namaste,

Rochel Marie Lawson, RN, AHP, CMS

The Queen of Feeling Fabulous

https://www.blissfulliving4u.com

https://www.unstoppable-womens-summit.com

https://www.facebook.com/rochele.lawson.5

https://www.instagram.com/rochelelawson

https://www.linkedin.com/in/rochelemarielawson

https://www.youtube.com/results?search_query=rochel+marie+lawson+channel

ACKNOWLEDGEMENTS

My deepest and most sincere thanks have to go to the Divine that created the essence, energy and opportunity to partake this venture on. Without the Divine bestowing upon me and leading me to be the woman that I am today, this project would not have been possible.

I love the Divine and my Divine team so much that words cannot convey the importance of all of them being an important part of my life. Everyday I wake up I give thanks for the blessings, challenges, lessons and wisdom that has guided me on this journey.

I give huge, heartfelt thanks to my children and family that have supported and put up with me. You are my inspiration to do and be better and to be that shining star that you see me as. I love you so very much!

I am deeply grateful to all of the women that I had a pleasure of speaking to during the implementation of this project. Without your grace and understanding the project would have not been a possibility.

I especially want to thank all the women that said yes to being a part of this project for putting your trust in me to lead us all in creating a legacy for the future females in our lineage. I have a deep appreciation for your love, grace, understanding and acceptance of me even if you did not know me. That warmed my heart and soul and I feel so much admiration and love for all of you.

My Blissful Living 4 U team. Without my team, I would not be able to do all that I do. Thank Fides, Nikka and Prati.

Lastly, I would like to thank all the fierce, fearless, unstoppable and Unf*ckwithable women that came before me. Without you laying the pathway for me to follow none of this would have been possible. Thank you for being true to yourself, your purpose in life and not letting anything stop you from achieving your dreams.

ABOUT THE AUTHOR

Rochel Marie Lawson known as the Queen of Feeling Fabulous is a co-founder of All Day Cable, Inc. a telecommunications installation company located in the heart of Silicon Valley and the founder and president of Blissful Living 4 U, both women-owned businesses. She is a trailblazer, motivator and leader that have been paving the way for other women to step into their greatness for over 30 years. She is a multiple #1 best selling author and international best selling author that gives her heart and soul in all that she sets out to do. She is a past president of NAWBO-Silicon Valley, past board of director of Sutter Health Hospital in Tracy, California, The Northern California Lupus Foundation, Sutter Health Foundation board member and relentless volunteer for organizations that support women and children. She is a Registered Nurse and has been licensed as a nurse for 30 years.

Rochel Marie spends her time between her beloved home state of California and San Antonio, Texas. She has 2 beautiful children, a Chihuahua named Diamond and an Australian Shepard named Beamer. She loves traveling the world, shopping for shoes, reading and spending time with her family. She is dedicated to uniting women around the world so that the world can become a better place. Learn more about Rochel Marie Lawson and how she unlocks bliss so that women and a few smart men can step into living the life of their dreams by balancing the pillars of wellness and wealth through wisdom at BlissfulLiving4U.com

https://www.blissfulliving4u.com

https://www.unstoppable-womens-summit.com

https://www.blissfulliving4u.com/podcast

BLISSFUL LIVING 4 U'S

THE BRAVE, BOLD, & UNSTOPPABLE
WOMEN'S SUMMIT™
Learn more at www.unstoppable-womens-summit.com

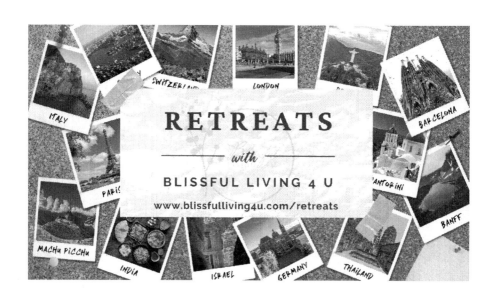

RETREATS

with

BLISSFUL LIVING 4 U

www.blissfulliving4u.com/retreats

Other Best Selling Books and Collaborative Books by Rochel Marie Lawson

Intro to Holistic Health Ayurveda Style

The Live Sassy Formula

Rapid Change for the Heart Centered Woman

Answering The Call

The Wellness Universe Guide to Complete Self-Care:
25 Tools for Stress Relief

The Wellness Universe Guide to Complete Self-Care:
25 Tools for Goddesses